Digital Dealing

Digital
Dealing

How e-Markets are Transforming the Economy

Robert E. Hall

 W. W. Norton & Company   New York London

Copyright © 2001 by Robert E. Hall

The text of this book is composed in Sabon
with the display set in Meta Normal
Composition by Gina Webster
Manufacturing by Quebecor World Fairfield
Book design by Chris Welch
Production manager: Andrew Marasia

Library of Congress Cataloging-in-Publication Data

Hall, Robert Ernest, 1943–
Digital dealing : how e-markets are transforming the economy /
Robert E. Hall.
p.   cm.
Includes index.
ISBN 0-393-04210-3
1. Electronic commerce. 2. Internet marketing. 3. Auctions—Computer net-
work resources. 4. Business enterprises—Computer networks. I. Title.
HF5548.32.H35 2001
381—dc21   2001030685

W. W. Norton & Company, Inc., 500 Fifth Avenue, New York, N.Y. 10110
www.wwnorton.com

W. W. Norton & Company Ltd., Castle House, 75/76 Wells Street,
London W1T 3QT

1 2 3 4 5 6 7 8 9 0

Contents

Preface

From childhood I've been fascinated by learning how things work. Anything related to computers was a particular target. I dreamed of owning a computer as a teenager and joined a small group of pioneer owners of home computers three years before the first PC hit the market. That machine weighed 80 pounds and had 64 K of memory and 256 K of disk. Its power was $\frac{1}{1000}$ that of the 2-pound Sony that I used to write most of this book.

Since 1995, the interesting use of the computer has been the Internet. The intensity of interest in the Internet where I live in Silicon Valley is breathtaking. Graduating M.B.A.'s at the Stanford Business School refuse to sign up for interviews with established East Coast companies—they all want to join Internet-related startups. Football, golf, and gossip have been forgotten as topics of conversation here. It's all the Internet, the new new thing.

Particularly exciting to the economist like myself is the use on the Internet of ideas about how to make deals that we previously thought were our own arcane secrets. Every day, eBay concludes several hundred thousand auctions using the principle that William Vickrey propounded more than 30 years ago. We regarded Vickrey as the Isaac Newton of auctions long before he received the Nobel Prize for his thinking, but we never thought his idea would launch a business worth more than $10 billion.

I decided to write this book because my research in this area had turned up a lot of information about how e-markets actually work that I thought would be useful to those active in Internet business. Nobody had tried to pull together the information about the different ways that deals are made on the Internet. In particular, large numbers of writers on Internet business seem to think that sellers just post prices on their web sites, and that all a buyer has to do is cruise among the sites to find the best price. Internet business is a lot more complex and interesting than that.

Most authors thank their families for staying out of their way when they write, but this book was born out of hundreds of conversations with my wife, Susan Woodward, and my son Chris. Susan taught me everything I know about electronic stock markets. She and Chris—employees of OffRoad Capital.com—got me involved in the design of OffRoad's private equity auctions. That experience was probably the single biggest factor leading to this book. We looked at every online auction we could find and thought carefully about how to adapt earlier experience to the particular business model of OffRoad. The resulting model—described in chapter 3—has priced more than a dozen private equity offerings.

Susan read the entire manuscript with her usual care and suggested many improvements from her perspective as an expert in these matters. Charlotte Pace, who runs my office at Stanford, read the entire manuscript from the intelligent laywoman's and professional editor's perspective, and also suggested many improvements.

I'm aware that parts of the book will be out of date soon. I've set up a web site on the topics of the book—www.Digital-Dealing.com. The web site contains the backup material that traditional books might provide as end-of-chapter notes. It tracks the changes that will no doubt overtake many of the companies discussed here. And it will have pictures of our beloved cat, the only family member not swept up in the new new thing.

1

The Essence of the Digital Deal

In e-markets, people make deals. Consumers buy books and sell Barbie dolls. Investors buy and sell stocks and bonds. Businesses buy steel ingots and sell bulldozers. Every transaction involves a deal—a determination of the price and quantity. Making deals is not easy, either in traditional commerce or in e-commerce. Whatever price the seller offers, the buyer will try for a lower price. Every market evolves customs and practices to streamline deal making and to overcome the gap between the hopes of the seller and of the buyer. A successful e-market automates deal making through the universal connectivity of the Internet. e-Markets displace traditional markets as they raise the efficiency of deal making.

Is Amazon the paradigm of e-commerce? When Wal-Mart starts to buy most of its products over the web, will it one-click offers from suppliers? Is finding the best price just a matter of searching enough web sites to find the lowest posted price?

The answer to these questions is *no*. In most e-commerce, the price emerges from some kind of dickering. Posted prices govern deals only in the markets where the Amazon model works: those for standardized products like CDs costing relatively little. Elsewhere, the buyer's reaction to a posted price is generally along the lines of "I don't pay the asking price." In most settings, only a chump pays the asking price, the list price, the rack rate, or whatever the posted price is called. e-Commerce—like all commerce—confronts a basic principle of deal making: *Conceal your best price.* When a seller meets a prospective buyer, the seller rarely leads with the best price that the seller is willing to sell for. When you buy a car, you know that the first price you hear about is not the best price you can get.

Buyers conceal their best prices as well. When you buy a car, you start the negotiations with a price lower than you know you will eventually pay. A deal is eventually made as the seller comes down closer to the seller's best price and the buyer moves up closer to the buyer's best price.

Traditionally, a lot of prices have been set by dickering or haggling or bargaining. As a rule of thumb in the modern American economy, the prices of retail products above $100 can be dickered. The price marked in the store is an asking price, not the best price. I learned this once when I was buying a tire at what I thought was a good price at a discount tire store. The clerk writing me up took a phone call from a guy who was proposing his own price for four tires, well below the advertised special. The clerk checked with the manager, whose answer was "Go for it." Lesson learned.

In traditional business-to-business transactions, dickering is universal and taken for granted. Procurement managers negotiate with suppliers. Neither begins the negotiation by revealing a best price. Hardly any procurement is done by ordering at posted prices. Anheuser-Busch doesn't one-click beer bottles from Owens-Illinois. The two companies negotiate intensively over price.

Amazon is an exception to the general rule of concealing the best price. As far as I know, you can't dicker with Amazon—

but I could be wrong, for reasons I will go into later. And Safeway, McDonald's, and many other retailers sell at their posted prices, without any room for dickering. These stores all sell standardized products at prices well under $100. But when there is more at stake, dickering breaks out. Successful e-markets don't suppress dickering; they provide an automated version of it.

> Successful e-markets support dickering.

Why Conceal Your Best Price?

Think about the example of serious dickering that most people have experienced—buying a car. First question: Why doesn't the salesperson just quote a price for the car you want, and stick to that price, in the same way that McDonald's quotes a fixed price for nine McNuggets? Why has Saturn failed to make uniform pricing stick? The answer is that the dealer can make more money by dickering, even though the process chews up time. With dickering, the dealer can get more profit from customers who don't demand good prices, while capturing the business of customers who insist on low prices.

Some car buyers abhor the process, want to get their new car as quickly as possible, and are willing to pay a higher price to avoid the pain. These people may be poorly informed about the likely best price as well. Other car buyers relish the process, do a huge amount of research, visit many dealers, call up brokers, and press for the very best price. A dealer makes the most money by extracting a high price from the first type while keeping the business of the second type. Selling the same product to customers at different prices is fundamental to profitable business.

Key to the success of the dealer's strategy of different prices for different customers is keeping the best price secret. Imagine what would happen if the actual price of each sale were published in the local paper. The customers who currently leave money on the table would be able to figure out what to ask for.

Different customers would begin to pay prices much closer to each other. The profit from extracting higher prices from some customers would disappear.

So the principle of concealing your best selling price is more than just setting an asking price or first offer at a high level. The seller needs to keep buyers in the dark about how much others are paying. Sellers will resist participating in markets where prices are published. This is a constraint on the design of e-commerce systems. Transparency—open knowledge of the prices of past transactions—is not a feature that all participants want. In a later chapter, I'll discuss the business model of Priceline, which never discloses anything about the prices that customers actually pay. To date, it is by far the most successful e-commerce site in attracting participation by unaffiliated large businesses, such as airlines. The Priceline model is so successful, in fact, that the airlines are planning to copy it, and the travel site Microsoft sponsored, Expedia, has licensed the model.

> It's often a good idea to keep deals secret.

Businesses go to great lengths to keep their deals secret. It is a common term of sale contracts—put in at the insistence of the seller—that the buyer may not disclose the terms. And when the buyer is a large organization, deals are often structured so that only the top management of the buying company knows the actual terms. It is a common practice to issue invoices at prices above actual prices. The difference is made up in a secret rebate handled only by top management.

In addition to keeping the prices of actual deals secret, sellers try to keep secret any information that would help buyers figure out the seller's rock-bottom price, determined by cost. In the car business, the actual cost of a car to a dealer is a closely guarded secret. It has little to do with the "dealer invoice" price. The dealer invoice price, like the sticker price of a car, is just a marketing number, set by carmakers for the convenience of their dealers. A process of Byzantine complexity sets the actual cost of a car to a dealer. Sellers love to create smoke screens that make customers think they are getting unusually good deals.

Posted prices often interact with dickering, especially when a large buyer is dickering with a seller of a large number of products. Grainger.com is a web site operated by a large established seller of MRO (maintenance, repair, and operations) products. On its site, Grainger offers posted prices, but these are not the prices that customers actually pay. Instead, a company like IBM dickers for a blanket discount on all of Grainger's products. The prices on Grainger's web site control what IBM pays without other customers' learning the prices that IBM actually pays. It would not be practical for IBM to dicker prices for each of the thousands of products it buys from Grainger. Similarly, Sears, Roebuck has a deal with United Airlines that lowers fares for Sears's employee travel below published levels. Sears's discount is a well-kept secret.

What about buyers? Do they care if deal terms leak out? If you buy a car, it does not matter much to you. But if you are a big company, the terms matter in two contradictory ways. You would like to use a favorable price you extracted from one seller to get a similar price from other sellers. But, on the other hand, you would like to get the best possible price from any particular seller by promising that seller complete secrecy. So purchasers generally keep prices secret, but give broad hints about good deals available from rivals when they are negotiating.

A broad principle is that *e-commerce does not change the fundamentals of deals*. The forces that make the players conceal their best prices are no different as the Internet improves communication. At the core of any successful e-commerce enterprise—outside of books, CDs, and groceries—will be a way to make deals happen despite the desire to conceal best prices.

Elements of an e-Commerce System

e-Commerce brings trading partners in touch with each other and helps them make deals. The simplest business model—Amazon's—presents product descriptions and prices, and customers choose whether or not to buy. There is no electronic version of dickering. Amazon has chosen to post its best price. In settings where players are unwilling to show their best prices, an e-commerce system needs to replace dickering with an electronic equivalent, or support dickering within the system. Many different solutions have emerged in e-commerce to solve this problem, both before the Internet and even more since the Internet propelled e-commerce to the center of attention.

An e-market is part of the bigger picture of e-commerce. The e-market won't succeed in diverting business from traditional markets unless it is part of strong e-commerce infrastructure. That infrastructure has four main parts: (1) ways for trading partners to find each other, (2) communication facilities and protocols for working out deals, (3) legal enforcement of contracts resulting from the deals, and (4) a communication system to tell other traders about the deal.

Thus e-commerce involves the following four steps:

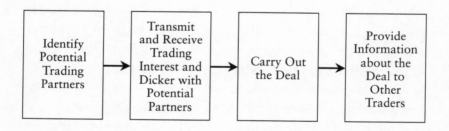

Identify Potential Trading Partners

Most businesses buy their inputs from thousands of vendors and sell to thousands of customers. They face the huge task of sifting through dozens of vendors for each of their inputs and of competing with dozens of rivals for the business of their customers. Traditional methods for getting in touch with suppliers and customers cut a lot of corners and leave potentially beneficial deals undone. The Internet improves the efficiency of tracking down trading partners because it permits vastly more efficient searches of information that is up-to-date.

One of the interesting questions about the process of locating trading partners is who takes the initiative. Should the buyer post a notice of interest in an exchange, or search among the offers posted by sellers? Should a seller take the initiative by searching the posted offers of buyers? Markets generally have customs about who takes the initiative—one side posts indications of interest, and the other searches actively. In traditional commerce, sellers generally take the initiative. IBM has a huge sales force, constantly calling on potential customers. In most companies, the sales people spend their time on the road, whereas the purchasing people are less numerous and stay at headquarters. The e-commerce analog is that the purchasing department posts requests for quotations, or RFQs, and potential suppliers search these RFQs. But, just as a good purchasing department will seek out suppliers who have not called on the department, an e-commerce system will support active searching by purchasers.

Transmit and Receive Trading Interest and Dicker with Potential Partners

Most of this book is about electronic dickering. Economics has a lot to say, in terms both of theory and of fact, about dickering. Automatic dickering was widespread long before it became electronic, in the form of auctions. Auctions come in many flavors. Bids may be sealed, as they are when the California government puts a highway contract out to bid, or they may be disclosed to other later bidders, as they are in a live auction for used cars or on eBay. One bidder may win everything, or many bidders may win. The winner may pay the price she bid, as in an antiques auction, or she may pay a lower price, as on eBay. Every combination of these design elements flourishes on the Internet.

Automatic dickering flourished before it became electronic.

Auctions are not the only form of electronic dickering. Many interesting alternatives flourished before the Internet, and others have taken root in the new soils of the Internet. For example, many business-to-business exchanges automate the sequence of posted RFQ, offers by suppliers in response, counteroffers, and acceptance.

Another answer to making deals is to collect offers to buy or sell and post them next to each other in an exchange. Although dickering does not occur, competition among the buyers or sellers forces them toward displaying their best prices. The Nasdaq stock market is the most conspicuous deal engine based on this principle. Another interesting application is eBay's Half.com, where you can choose among dozens of posted offers for a used CD.

Finalize the Deal

Once automated dickering is over, the parties actually carry out their transaction. It is essential that this step be rock solid. A lot of the serious details of e-commerce relate to this back end. If there is significant value at stake, the parties need either to trust one another or to use an escrow to be sure that both sides perform. Users of eBay are familiar with the sinking feeling they have when they send off their money, trusting an unknown seller to ship their baseball tickets in return. Modern economies have elaborate commercial infrastructure to handle transactions once the terms have been dickered. The infrastructure is being adapted and extended to apply to e-commerce. This book does not cover finalization—that's a topic for a lawyer more than an economist.

> It is essential that all players not be allowed to back out.

It is, however, essential that all players in automated dickering know that the deal they make will actually take place—that they are committed and cannot back out. Otherwise, sham participation in dickering is a way to get information about the other side's best price. The worst outrage in buying a car is to dicker a price with the salesman and then learn that the sales manager has turned it down.

There is a close relation between the finalization step in e-commerce and the first step of identifying potential trading partners. Only the partners that can be trusted to follow through on a deal should go on the list. e-Commerce systems involve certifying participants and issuing credentials to this end.

Provide Information about the Deal to Other Traders

I've already mentioned conflicts over broadcasting information about deals. Transparency—speedy disclosure of deals for the benefit of other traders—is an abstract ideal advocated by many commentators on e-commerce. But transparency is not in the interest of some players, and it may not even be good for the market as a whole.

Publication of prices is a help to other traders in general. If you are planning to build a house, it helps you to know what has been paid to build similar houses in your area recently. If you could find out what people had paid for a flight from Detroit to Minneapolis, it would help you formulate your bid on Priceline. But publication is sometimes harmful to a particular trader. Northwest Airlines does not want its Priceline fares to be published, because the airline would lose the profit it currently makes from sales to people who bid above the lowest fare Northwest will accept.

Business-to-Business e-Markets

For a few months around the end of 1999, B-to-B hysteria swept American financial markets. Startups with B-to-B business plans—Ventro, FreeMarkets, and Ariba, to name a few—gained billions of dollars of stock market valuation long before they earned any profit. Then values tumbled in the spring and fall of 2000. The actual development of business transactions on the

Internet progressed smoothly during that period and after the crash. There is little doubt about the importance of the Internet for B-to-B; the ups and downs of market capitalizations of B-to-B players reveal changing beliefs about how much money will be made from what is sure to be a large volume of business.

Captive B-to-B e-markets are beating out neutral e-markets.

A particularly important question about B-to-B is how much trading will occur in neutral, independently owned e-markets, and how much in e-markets operated by existing large players. A good part of the story of the crash was the finding that neutrals were making little headway against the e-markets set up by big companies or consortiums. Providers of B-to-B infrastructure such as Ariba and CommerceOne prospered because they found good markets for their products among the captive e-markets. The largest player, FreeMarkets, grew rapidly by providing consulting and software services to large companies establishing their own procurement e-markets.

The Variety of e-Markets

The job of an e-market is to make deals by overcoming buyers' and sellers' reluctance to reveal their best prices. At the heart of an e-market is its deal engine. eBay's engine is a neat adaptation of the traditional English auction. Nasdaq's engine based on posting and acceptance of electronic offers to buy and sell is suited to the high speed of the stock market. An e-market's deal engine automates the process of making a deal between a seller whose initial price offer is higher than the seller's best price and a buyer whose initial offer is lower than the buyer's best price. The engine finds an acceptable price somewhere in between, and a quantity of the product as well.

Many Internet deal engines run electronic auctions. Others allow customers to select from offerings from a variety of sellers.

And the simplest of all is the e-market where a customer chooses whether or not to pay the price posted by the seller. The choice among these models is not random, but rather depends on the nature of the product and the roles of the players. The six primary e-market models are the following:

1. **The eBay model.** The product is one of a kind, and there are several interested buyers. The seller wants to get one buyer to pay something close to her highest price. The seller arranges for the buyers to bid against each other in an automated auction.
2. **The OffRoad model.** One seller offers multiple units of the same product. Many buyers bid against each other, and those with the highest bids receive the units.
3. **The FreeMarkets model.** The product is a component specified by the buyer, not used by others, and there are several potential suppliers. The buyer arranges for the suppliers to bid against each other in a buy-side or reverse auction.
4. **The Nasdaq model.** The product is standardized, with many buyers and sellers. They meet in an exchange, where both buyers and sellers can post offers and consider offers from others.
5. **The Priceline model.** The product normally trades in a market where some buyers pay much higher prices than others. To make even lower prices available without alerting the customers who pay higher prices, customers willing to accept restrictions can make their own offers. Sellers accept or reject the offers from customers.
6. **The Grainger model.** The seller specifies the product and makes it in volume. There are several or many buyers. The seller posts an asking price and may dicker with customers over blanket discounts (Grainger) or may not dicker at all (Amazon).

The eBay Model: Auctions for a Single Item

The workhorse deal engine is the auction. Auctions made deals for hundreds of years. They moved to electronic form well before the Internet took over—the U.S. Treasury auctioned billions of dollars of bonds for many years electronically. Auctions fit so naturally on the Internet that auction volume there has reached startling levels—in 2000, Internet auctions made deals for more than a trillion dollars in goods and securities.

Briefly, here's how an auction solves the problem of making a deal between a seller and alternative buyers, when all the players want to conceal their best prices. Frank wants to sell his Camaro, and Paul, Juanita, and Yoriko are interested in buying it. Frank will take $10,000 for it, but the buyers don't know that and Frank is not telling, because he hopes for more. Paul will pay up to $9,000 for it, but also is not telling, because he hopes (unrealistically) for a lower price. Juanita will pay up to $12,000 and Yoriko up to $11,000.

> Auctions get the players to reveal their best prices.

Frank decides to run a standard English auction. He gathers the three potential buyers in a room and asks for bids. He sets the rule that each bid must be at a price $500 or more above the most recent bid. The auction is over when nobody wants to raise the bid, and the Camaro goes to the last (and highest) bidder. The bidding goes as follows:

Bidder	Bid	Comment
Paul	$8,000	
Yoriko	8,500	
Paul	9,000	
Juanita	9,500	Paul is now priced out of the auction
Yoriko	10,000	
Juanita	10,500	
Yoriko	11,000	
Juanita	11,500	Yoriko is now priced out of the auction so Juanita wins at this price

Paul dropped out when the price passed his cutoff of $9,000; Yoriko, when the price passed her cutoff of $11,000. Juanita got her Camaro for less than her cutoff price of $12,000.

Suppose that Frank had said that the bid increment was $100 rather than $500. There would have been a lot more bids and the auction would have taken longer, but the result would have been similar: Juanita would be the winner because Yoriko would have dropped out when the price went over her cutoff of $11,000. Juanita would pay $11,100. There is a general rule of auctions: *the winner is the player with the highest cutoff price, and the winner pays the runner-up's cutoff price plus (possibly) the bid increment.* I say "possibly" here because sometimes the winner pays just the second-highest cutoff price without the increment. Suppose Juanita had bid $11,000 instead of $10,500. She would have won at that price because Yoriko would not bid $11,500, the next permissible bid.

Most of the auctions considered in the next chapter obey this rule or something like it.

An auction is formalized dickering. To see this, suppose Frank had put the three buyers in separate rooms and dickered separately. Each time he got an offer from one, he would take it to the others to beat. The highest offer he could possibly get to take to Juanita would be Yoriko's cutoff of $11,000. So Juanita could offer something over $11,000 and get her Camaro. Both the identity of the buyer and the price (roughly) are the same with the auction or the dickering.

We can't say just what the dickered price would be. Economics does not have a precise theory of dickering. If Frank is the better bargainer, he might be able to push Juanita close to her maximum value of $12,000, or maybe she is the tough one and can keep Frank close to his best alternative, selling the car to Yoriko for her cutoff price of $11,000.

As chapter 2 will show, economics does not have a precise theory of auctions either. The example here is contrived in one important way—it is based on the idea that the players all have cutoff prices firmly in mind before the auction begins. In fact, there is lots of evidence that people learn during auctions and adjust their ideas about the value of what is for sale.

eBay brought the auction deal engine to millions of consumers who had no contact with auctions before—the stuff initially sold on eBay traded previously in flea markets with informal dickering. Before eBay, auctions for collectibles were important only for the more valuable high-end objects. Real-time auctions for art, antiques, and wine were expensive to run and expensive to attend. eBay cut these costs to practically zero and opened up the possibility of auctions for all kinds of additional stuff.

eBay did much more than automate auctions and make them close to free to operate and attend. It popularized the electronic version of a device sometimes used earlier in physical auctions, the proxy bid. You inform eBay secretly of the highest bid you are willing to make, and eBay keeps your visible bid one tick above any other bid, until it reaches your limit. You stay in the auction without having to check the eBay web site. By this method, eBay implements the idea that gave William Vickrey the Nobel Prize in economics. More on this in the next chapter.

e-Markets came later to B-to-B commerce than to consumer markets and securities trading. One of the most successful players in B-to-B is eBay, whose auctions for surplus equipment generate far greater volume than do many e-markets aimed solely at this business. The eBay auction model suits the task of liquidating equipment splendidly.

The OffRoad Model: Stocks and Bonds

Many e-markets use auctions for multiple identical objects. OffRoad Capital auctions shares in developing companies before they go public. Other e-markets auction the stocks of companies going public or auction bonds. The deal engines in the stock market and the bond market always auction many units, generally to many bidders. An interesting question is whether the winning bidders should pay the prices they bid, or whether they should all pay the same price. e-Markets vary in this choice. The U.S. Treasury changed its rule in 1998 to a single-price auction for its bonds, after years of heckling from economists critical of its earlier pay-your-own-bid auctions.

Growth of Internet auctions of securities has been rapid. One organization alone—MuniAuction—masterminds auctions of over a trillion dollars a year of municipal and government agency bonds. These are pure B-to-B deals—the public is not allowed to bid. OffRoad auctions the stock of private companies to investors on its web site. The OffRoad deal engine has some interesting features discussed in chapter 3. Another web-based investment bank, W. R. Hambrecht, holds auctions for companies doing IPOs—the auction helps determine the price where the stock begins to trade in Nasdaq.

> The non-auction deal engine powers some kinds of e-markets, such as Nasdaq.

The Nasdaq Model: Exchanges with Many Buyers and Sellers

The auction deal engine does not monopolize e-markets, however. Huge volumes of deals—also in the trillions of dollars per year—are made in exchanges. The Nasdaq stock exchange is the biggest. Participants in Nasdaq—professional traders and dealers, pension and mutual funds, and individual investors—post offers to trade on the Nasdaq network. Participants can also peruse the existing offers and accept one that is attractive. Nasdaq does not support electronic dickering, though plenty of dickering occurs on the phone. The advantage of the no-dickering real-time deal engine is speed. You can make a deal on the Nasdaq system in two seconds.

> The advantage of the no-dickering real-time deal engine is speed.

When a deal engine does not provide automated dickering for individual deals, a pair of players will often negotiate blanket discounts that cover all deals between themselves. In Nasdaq, for example, a mutual fund will take all of its business in certain stocks to one market maker, in exchange for a negotiated discount of a few cents per share.

eBay's subsidiary Half.com runs a copy of Nasdaq for used books, CDs, and videos. You can peruse the listings for hundreds of thousands of different titles and choose from among dozens of competing offers. As in Nasdaq, there is no dickering, but plenty of pressure on sellers to offer good prices—somebody offering $8 for an Eminem CD in excellent condition can't expect to make a sale if there are lots of offers at $7. Competition takes the place of dickering in persuading sellers to sell at close to their best prices.

Supply-chain commodities—steel, chemicals, plastic—seem appropriate for an active e-market exchange where prices change every day to balance supply and demand. At least that is the hope of eSteel, ChemConnect, and PlasticsNet. None has yet generated enough volume to prove that a neutral exchange can replace the existing informal market.

In e-market exchanges where both buyers and sellers can post offers, there is likely to be a disproportion of one or the other: ChemConnect has 2.5 times as many sell offers as buy offers, for example.

e-Market theorists like to praise neutral exchanges, where the computer can match long lists of buyers to long lists of sellers. And some exist, like Nasdaq, still the largest e-market. But the likelihood seems to favor e-markets sponsored by the buyer or the seller, whichever is larger. Big companies will establish captive procurement e-markets, either by themselves or through consortiums such as Covisint, the e-market purchasing partnership formed by GM, Ford, and Daimler-Chrysler. Where the product suits an e-market selling model—as in air travel—the large player will also operate a captive sell-side e-market, as the airlines do (Orbitz). The future of the neutral exchange is cloudy.

The Priceline Model: Price Offers from Customers

Priceline and its licensee, the travel web site Expedia, operate e-markets fine-tuned to meet the needs of airlines, car rental

companies, and hotels. These companies sell perishable products—space in planes or hotels, or the services of rental cars. The
aim is to sell the products to customers who can pay only low
prices, without giving the same low prices to business customers
willing to pay much higher prices. A Priceline customer may pay
$150 for a seat next to an executive paying $950. The Priceline
deal engine operates in real time without automated dickering. A
customer makes a price offer and the sellers either accept it or
reject it.

A key feature of the Priceline model is that prices remain
secret. Business travelers looking for good prices can't find them
at Priceline or at Expedia's Price Matcher. The only way to determine what price might be available is to formulate a bid and see
what happens. Because of this requirement and the fact that you
have to accept early departures, inconvenient connections, and
late arrivals, few business travelers will use the model—exactly
the goal of the model.

The FreeMarkets Model: Business-to-Business Procurement

B-to-B e-markets can automate dickering in the supply chain.
The products bought here are built into the purchaser's own
product. FreeMarkets is the leading supplier of e-market infrastructure for procurement. Its clients run auctions for tens of billions of dollars in components and other inputs. Much
supply-chain commerce involves components designed specifically for the purchaser. These will never trade in an open market
like a commodity. But an e-market can organize dickering over
the prices of the components. For example, Ford uses auction
processes for components such as plastic moldings or steel forg-
ings. In a procurement auction, potential sellers bid against each
other to be the supplier. As each one bids a better deal for the
purchaser, the price declines—so procurement auctions are often
called *reverse auctions* because the price moves in the opposite
direction from a sell-side auction.

In supply-chain e-commerce, it remains to be seen who will

operate the surviving exchanges. Will it be purchasers, either individually or in industrial alliances like the auto industry's Covisint? Will it be the component suppliers, also possibly in an alliance? Or will the winner be an independent, neutral exchange? So far, the odds seem to favor larger firms, typically the purchasers, over suppliers and neutrals.

The Grainger Model: Posted Prices with Blanket Discounts

Another segment of B-to-B commerce is the supply of hundreds of thousands of MRO (maintenance, repair, and operations) products such as mops, cleaning solutions, nuts and bolts, and computer paper. Here the successful model is plainly the online catalog plus blanket discount. Grainger neatly transported its established MRO business from a paper catalog and phone-order model to the corresponding web model. Grainger negotiates blanket discounts for each corporate customer, covering hundreds of thousands of maintenance and repair products. An extension of the same model is Dell Premium, where Dell creates a unique e-market for a single corporate customer. Product selection and prices are negotiated centrally, and then the customer's employees can order individually from the Premium site at the negotiated prices.

> Posted prices with dickered blanket discounts form an effective model in some e-markets.

The posted-price model avoids the burden of automated negotiations through auctions. The employees who handle participation in auctions need considerable responsibility to make decisions about how much to bid. In markets where prices change only slowly and the product specification is familiar to both buyer and seller, the posted-price model makes more sense. Employees handling these transactions do not have any price-setting responsibility—they only determine the quantity purchased.

The rule of concealing your best price applies in MRO and other types of purchasing where posted prices are the logical way to handle the transactions. In some cases, where the volume of purchasing is too small to merit overcoming the rule, B-to-B transactions occur at rack prices. Many businesses buy small numbers of books from Amazon, for example, without trying to get better prices. I call this the strict posted-price model.

For higher-volume MRO purchases, a company leaves money on the table if it does not negotiate with a posted-price seller for a blanket discount. The quoted price on the web is not the best price. Most of these deals are kept as deep secrets, but some are public. Grainger gives the federal government free shipping and 10 to 15 percent off the prices quoted on its web site.

A single blanket discount is the simplest way around the fact that posted prices are never best prices. e-Markets have much more elaborate solutions as well. MRO vendors and companies like Dell will establish special prices for each of their products for large customers. In effect, there is a special web site for each customer.

Transparency

In a transparent e-market, everybody knows everything about bids and deals. Most commentators on e-markets see transparency as an unquestioned good idea. But it's actually a tough issue. There are all kinds of dimensions to the information that might be shown to e-market participants. Actual practices in e-markets run all the way from complete secrecy about deals, at one end, to immediate display of every detail on a web site, at the other end.

The issues of transparency fall into three categories:

1. **Identity of traders.** What should bidders learn about the organization offering to sell or buy? What should the players learn about the bidders?
2. **Terms of bids.** What should the players learn about pending bids? Should they be given information during the dickering, or only afterwards?

3. **Terms of the deal.** What should the players learn about the resulting deal?

To illustrate, here is FreeMarkets' answer to transparency. The buyer sponsoring a procurement auction knows a great deal about the bidders, because they first go through a bidder qualification process where the auction sponsor checks their credentials. A bidder does not know other bidders' identities, either during the auction or afterwards. Bidders know the prices bid by other bidders in time to respond during the auction. Nothing is ever disclosed about the terms of the actual deal.

eBay's transparency is quite different. You can learn the eBay name and email address of the seller and all the bidders at any time. You can check the feedback about any of them. The only information about bids during an auction is the current auction price. Because the current price may be below the maximum price of the leading bidder, you don't know how much you would have to bid in order to become the winner. Also, you can't find out about the most important bids, those that come in at the last second. After the auction closes, eBay publishes the maximum prices of all bidders except the winner. You can find the winning price and identity of the winning bidder on eBay by displaying the closed auctions in the product category that interests you.

Identity of Traders

In a sell-side auction, bidders benefit from knowing the identity of the seller. First, they care about the reputation of the seller for describing the product accurately and for delivering it as promised. Second, sellers may have special knowledge that makes buying from them dangerous. In the stock market, this problem is common, because of inside information. An insider at a company may be selling because he knows the secret that the company has lost an important customer. As a buyer, you would like to know whether the seller is an insider or just another outside investor.

Sellers may prefer anonymity. A seller whom buyers might suspect of adverse inside information will choose to be anonymous. On the other hand, a seller without access to inside information—like a pension fund in the stock market—wants to advertise its identity.

As a general matter, a trader is attracted to an e-market if the other traders must disclose their identities, but this trader has the option of disclosure or anonymity. But e-markets can't be all things to all people. In Nasdaq, those who want to know whom they are trading with take their business out of the e-market—they trade personally over the phone. Trades in the e-market through dealers are partially anonymous—the dealer knows what broker a trade comes from, but not the identity of the customer.

A key factor favoring concealing the identity of bidders in a sell-side or a buy-side auction is discouraging collusion among the bidders. If one bidder in a procurement auction sees a particular rival pushing the price down, the bidder can call up the rival and propose to eliminate the competition by dividing the market in advance.

In a captive B-to-B e-market, the identity of the company sponsoring an auction is known for sure, or is known to be a member of a consortium. As a general rule in those markets, the identities of the bidders—would-be suppliers or purchasers—are not disclosed at any time. I believe the primary motivation for secrecy is to discourage collusion among the bidders.

> Secrecy about deals discourages collusion among the bidders.

In independent exchanges, the general custom is to keep the identities of potential traders secret until the deal is made. An important motivation in this case is to force the parties to make their deal on the exchange and to pay its fees. On eBay, where all parties are identified before the auction closes, it is common for the seller to propose an off-eBay deal, to limit the fee that eBay earns. eBay's rule against this scam is hard to enforce.

Terms of Bids

In an *open-book* auction, bidders know the prices offered by other bidders and can rebid in response. An open-book auction achieves its purpose only if there is a mechanism for giving all bidders a chance to respond to every bid. Some auctions have a *going, going, gone* procedure for this purpose. The auction does not close until all bidders have remained silent for a designated period, but none choose to respond. Some of the largest Internet auctions, including MuniAuction (municipal bonds) and eBay, have nominal open books but no going, going, gone, so all bids come in the last few seconds and the book is effectively closed.

> Most B-to-B e-markets have opted for open books.

Most B-to-B e-markets have opted for open books. The standard FreeMarkets auction displays bids in real time and does not close until a full minute passes without any bid. Auctions for used equipment and surplus merchandise generally do the same.

Terms of Deals

It's helpful to other participants in an e-market to learn the prices paid in earlier transactions. The public interest in disclosure may not coincide with the interests of the sponsor of an e-market. Visteon, a large maker of car parts, can extract the lowest price from a supplier of plastic moldings by keeping the price secret, but other buyers and sellers of similar moldings would benefit from knowing that price. In the stock market, the public interest acts through the Securities and Exchange Commission, the regulator of the stock market. It is illegal for anyone but private individuals to trade stocks without reporting the trade ("printing the trade," as they say on Wall Street) to the New York Stock Exchange, Nasdaq, or another exchange.

Although other players would love to know the terms of deals, the balance favors keeping the terms secret in many cases. Even in the stock market, the requirement for printing trades makes it easy for dealers to see what their rivals are up to. If the dealers in a stock make an agreement to keep the spreads wide, they are much more likely to spot cheaters and enforce the agreement if they all can see the terms of each trade.

In a procurement consortium such as the auto industry's Cov-isint, secrecy about trades is virtually mandatory. First, the members of the consortium compete with each other and do not want their rivals to know about their costs. Second, as chapter 7 will discuss, antitrust law frowns on any arrangement where a group of companies work jointly to depress prices paid to sup-pliers—this violates the same laws that forbid conspiracies to charge customers high prices. To pass antitrust muster, a consor-tium must have convincing firewalls isolating one member from another.

Competition and Profits in e-Markets

e-Markets have the power to transform the economy. It's much easier to shop and buy on the Internet than on foot. Not only can you check prices by visiting sellers' sites, but you can also use shopping bots such as mySimon that check them all for you and put all the prices for an object on one page. It seems that compe-tition should be sharper, and prices and profits lower, in the new economy with e-markets than in the old economy. And it would seem that a seller whose prices were above the best prices found by the bots would sell little.

It turns out the e-market equilibrium is more complex and interesting than the prediction of cutthroat competition enforced by shopping bots. In the first place, bots do nothing to overcome the unwillingness of sellers to reveal their best prices. A bot can't tell you what price you will pay after you dicker, nor can it pre-dict the price you would pay in an auction. At best, bots help you buy books and CDs and other low-priced, standardized products sold at fixed prices without dickering. Bots have no useful role in markets for stocks and bonds, collectibles, used

equipment, industrial commodities, custom-specified components, or the other areas where e-markets are flourishing.

Despite the helpful bots, prices in e-markets where the bots
can find prices, such as books, have not fallen to a uniformly low
level. On the contrary, you have a choice between high-service,
high-price outlets such as Amazon or low-service, low-price ones
such as 1BookStreet. You will find particularly
high prices at niche online bookstores such as
FatBrain.

> The zero-profit principle is indispensable in understanding market equilibrium.

Future profit drives market equilibrium. If
prospects are favorable in one e-market, startups
will target the market. Priceline's success spawned
several important rivals. With more players in a
market, prospective profit falls. In equilibrium, a
potential new player won't get funded and enter
the business, because the future profit falls a little
short of the current investment. The market for cheap surplus
airplane seats and hotel rooms may be approaching this zero-
profit point. Online bookstores are already there. The *zero-profit
principle* holds that new sellers will enter a market until the
prospective profit (in excess of the normal return to capital) is
zero.

The zero-profit principle is indispensable in understanding
market equilibrium. Unless a pioneer in an e-market has a powerful patent or builds up a real head start like eBay's, its profit
will erode as others enter the market. In a line of business where
there are too many players for any to profit, some will leave the
business, and the profit of the survivors will rise to make them
viable.

e-Markets will sort customers by convenience and value of
time as well. Travelers willing to search the Internet for bargains
and to take flights with inconvenient times and connections will
continue to get vastly lower fares than the full-fare business traveler. Priceline is only one of a number of e-market devices that
help airlines segment their markets. Airlines operate e-markets
on their own web sites and on computer reservation systems.

The airlines aim to fill up seats at low prices that would otherwise be empty. Chapter 6 tracks fares for ten flights leaving the same day, over the month before the flights left. The results show that airlines have mastered the fine-tuning of fares. This could happen only in an e-market.

e-Market equilibrium often involves secondary markets. Here people trade products after producers have sold them to their direct customers. Secondary markets thrive in particular when there is mispricing in the primary market. Sports teams generally underprice their best tickets (don't ask me why). eBay runs a vast secondary market in those tickets. Although the stock market is a secondary market for registered companies, there is room for a big expansion of secondary e-markets in other securities, such as corporate bonds and shares in unregistered companies. Regulations against these secondary markets are relaxing, and they are sure to grow rapidly.

e-Market equilibrium also involves dealers. These range from the Wall Street professional to the eBay coin trader. Dealers buy on e-markets at low prices and sell on the same markets at higher prices. Their activities obey the zero-profit principle—if opportunities to trade profitably are widespread, more dealers enter and they compete down the profits. If prices are so tight that opportunities to buy low and sell high are rare, dealers will leave the market and prices will loosen, keeping the remaining dealers at the zero-profit point. Because trading on e-markets is so much cheaper than in traditional markets, the opening up of e-markets has expanded opportunities for dealers. The coin market knew much smaller numbers of small-time traders when trading meant visiting stores and finding people. eBay spawned a new community of these traders.

Dealers flourish in many e-markets.

The wild expansion of Internet commerce in digital music calls attention to another feature of market equilibrium, the price-volume tradeoff. Every seller in every market faces the tradeoff. At a high price, volume will be low but the profit margin on each unit will be high. Conversely, at a low price, volume is high but margin low. Profit is volume multiplied by margin. The two elements move in opposite directions. It may be a close call whether to use a high-price, low-volume strategy or a low-price, high-volume strategy. The traditional recorded-music business adopted a mixture, selling CDs at high prices and low volumes, but selling the same music over the radio at low prices and high volumes.

The music industry kept the two outlets segmented until the Internet upset this model. Although it is possible to record music off the air on a cassette, lost CD business from that source was not a serious constraint on the low-price broadcast strategy. Record companies recognized that broadcast was a big factor in promoting CD sales. So far, the companies have not figured out how to put Internet digital music into their model. They have made a few attempts to enforce the high-price, low-volume strategy by selling digital tracks at prices equivalent to CD prices, but the resulting volume has been low. The music business will probably evolve toward a low-price, high-volume strategy for Internet MP3s, but it may take a while.

Government Policy

Modern governments let markets thrive without much supervision. The government establishes basic infrastructure—enforcement of contracts and punishment of fraud—but leaves the rest to market participants. As the most modern of markets, e-markets enjoy this benign neglect most fully.

The government does concern itself with abuses that limit competition. The government wields two closely related tools—antitrust laws and regulation—to step in where competition has failed in a way that can be corrected.

Two long-established e-markets—airline computer reservation systems and the Nasdaq stock market—are natural laboratories for studying government protection of competition. The government found that the airlines were using the apparatus associated with the reservation systems to negotiate fare increases with each other. A court order under antitrust law stopped the practice. The government also found that the big airlines that operated the reservations systems discriminated against smaller airlines that were customers of those systems. The remedy was a complex set of regulations preventing discrimination.

In Nasdaq, the government found that dealers were harassing other dealers to try to dissuade them from making better offers to investors to buy or sell stocks. Not only did the government insist on measures to detect and prevent these abuses, but it also imposed many new rules on Nasdaq. Before the new rules went into effect, individual investors in Nasdaq stocks could transact only through the dealers, who would buy low and sell high on every transaction. Now traders on Nasdaq can, if they choose, see offers to trade from many other traders and frequently trade directly with each other. Dealers still buy low and sell high, but have lost their monopoly on trading.

The government is looking carefully at new e-markets where—as in the airline and Nasdaq cases—the facilities of the e-markets bring competitors into contact with each other. The government approved the Covisint e-market created by major American carmakers after being assured that Covisint had adequate firewalls to prevent collusion that would harm suppliers or car buyers.

Government regulation of e-markets is not always wise. For example, most states flatly outlaw the sale of new cars on the Internet by carmakers. The regulation reflects the political clout of car dealers protecting their monopoly in car retailing. The consumer would benefit from a fair fight between dealers and direct Internet sales to see which is better.

Patents and Copyrights

e-Market designers have applied for patents on new methods for operating e-markets. The government has issued a number of important patents. In particular, Priceline holds a patent on its method for letting customers enter bids that businesses accept selectively. Amazon holds a patent on one-click shopping.

Patents provide the incentive to innovate in e-markets as in other lines of business. Without patents, the developer of a new e-market tool might become the victim of the zero-profit principle, as copycats invaded the market and drove prices down. But business methods patents in e-markets are controversial—there is almost a consensus that they are harmful because they stand in the way of innovation by others. It is too early to judge the issue, because the actual effect of the patents remains incompletely tested. Microsoft and Priceline fought over Microsoft's use of Priceline's patented customer bidding system in its travel site, Expedia. The dispute ended when Expedia paid for a license to use the patent—the court did not have a chance to rule on the issue.

Copyrights are important in e-markets for two reasons. First, e-markets are uniquely efficient in selling digital information products—MP3s, e-books, videos—and all are protected by copyrights. The owner of the copyright controls the copying of the information. Without this control, ownership has no value, because others can supply copies at close to zero cost. The challenge is to create an e-market business model that respects copyrights but still does a good job of distributing the products.

The second role of copyrights is to protect the value created by the owners of e-markets. The information about current and closed auctions on eBay, for example, is the valuable property of eBay. Although eBay makes the information available for free to its customers and visitors, it retains property rights in it. eBay can exclude other businesses from copying information in gobs off its site. When BiddersEdge copied eBay's auction information and displayed the information on its own site, eBay went successfully to court to block BiddersEdge. Similarly, independent exchanges trading Nasdaq stocks such as Instinet are resisting Nasdaq's attempts to copy critical information for free from their systems to display it on the Nasdaq system.

e-Markets generate information, and information is property. With property rights secured by copyright, information owners can choose the way information is distributed to their rivals and to the public. It is undesirable to undermine information property rights for the same reason it is undesirable to undermine rights in music, books, or movies—valuable property rights create incentives to create value in the first place.

Implications

The Internet is a powerful new tool for distributing information. Whatever the gyrations of the market values of e-market companies, consumers and businesses will make more and more deals on the Internet. e-Markets will continue growing fast.

New e-markets will flourish if they are more successful than their traditional and electronic rivals in solving the basic problem of commerce—inducing potential traders to move from their first offered prices to something closer to the best prices they are willing to offer to a trading partner. Some will automate dickering with an auction, some will formalize it with an RFQ-offer-counteroffer process, some will resemble Nasdaq with an offer-accept model with blanket discounts, and some will offer catalogs with negotiated prices.

> Whatever the gyrations of the market values of e-market companies, e-markets will continue to grow fast.

Auctions will predominate for collectibles, surplus equipment, industrial commodities, many securities, and sports and airline tickets. Reverse auctions will take over the procurement of low-tech industrial components. Auctions are favored when there is a lot of uncertainty about the market value of the objects. The value has to be high enough to make the auction process worthwhile, and the players need to have enough time to make the auction work. Auctions will have open books and going, going, gone processes if it is useful for bidders to learn about other bids and respond intelligently to them. e-Market designers will choose closed books or at least permit last-minute bids without going, going, gone if they hope to attract experts who do not want to show their hands to others.

The RFQ-offer-counteroffer e-market model suits B-to-B commerce in neutral exchanges. The Nasdaq offer-accept e-market model is likely to be the winner when traders are in a hurry or it is not worth the time to dicker. An e-market based on this model works best if it can display numerous competing offers for the same object on the same screen, as Nasdaq and Half.com do. In that case, competition among the offerers pushes them toward displaying their best prices to the public.

Finally, catalogs with prices crafted to the buyer will predominate in settings like MRO or computers where the buyer plans large volumes of transactions initiated by many different people for thousands of different products.

In the standard auction model, deals are made at a specified time—usually a few days or weeks after the announcement of the auction. In many settings, auctions occur on a regular schedule—Treasury bills every week, basic metals every day at Metal-Site. In those settings, e-markets function periodically. When you decide you want to trade, you have to wait for the next auction closing to have a chance to buy. Procurement auctions for a particular type of component at one large business may occur once every year or two, as the outcome is a supply contract of that duration.

The Internet version of the traditional auction is a mainstay of e-markets. Hundreds of software suppliers, including mighty Microsoft, sell auction software to e-market sponsors. Other suppliers, such as Perfect.com, are application service providers; they host e-markets for customers on their own servers. In any of its variations—sealed bid versus open book, first price versus second price, one item versus many items, seller versus buyer sponsorship—the electronic auction solves the basic problem of getting the players to reveal their best prices.

- **Conceal your best price.** As a buyer, don't pay the asking price. As a seller, don't set your first offer to the lowest you are willing to accept. Be ready to dicker. Choose an e-market business model that harnesses the value of dickering.

- **Build your e-market within a robust e-commerce infrastructure.** An e-market depends on systems for locating trading partners, for ensuring payment, and for delivering products.

- **Choose an e-market business model suited to your business.** Use auctions for selling used equipment or collectibles and for securities whose value is uncertain. Use procurement auctions for supply-chain purchases that don't require long-term relationships. Use a real-time exchange if products or securities are standardized and speed is important. Use posted prices and blanket discounts for catalog sales.

- **Make an intelligent choice about transparency.** Open your auction book if the presence of some bidders helps others formulate their bids. Give bidders incentives to place bids early. Be careful not to let transparency lead to collusion.

- **Recognize the role of secondary markets and dealers.** These markets and players will spring up whenever there is an opportunity to buy low and sell high.

- **Recognize that competition will limit your profits.** Rivals will enter e-market competition up to the point where the profit anticipated by the next player into the business will be zero. As this entry occurs, the profits of existing participants will fall, though not necessarily to zero.

2

Auction Deal Engines

Online business requires a deal engine. The engine automates the process of deal making between a buyer and a seller. The simplest engine is the Amazon-style click and order at a posted price. But more complex engines power most e-commerce. Because the buyer conceals the highest price the buyer is willing to pay and the seller conceals the lowest price the seller will accept, a deal engine generally is needed to bring about a meeting of the minds between buyer and seller.

Deal engines fall into two categories. One is the auction. MetalSite runs an auction on most business days at 10:00 A.M. eastern time for many types of raw metal. The Tokyo stock exchange auctions stocks four times a day. These auctions are periodic. Others occur randomly, as sellers or buyers decide to launch them. All auctions result in deals at isolated moments in time. The second category of deal engine operates in real time; it creates continuing flows of deals. The Nasdaq stock market is a leading example. We will look at auctions in this chapter and the next two and at exchanges with real-time deal engines in chapter 5.

The Basic Auction Engine

The English auction introduced in the first chapter is the leading example of a deal engine. For centuries, the English auction has served in thousands of places to automate dickering. I'll start this chapter with a close look at the English auction as it operates on the Internet. eBay has made the English auction famous on the web and accounts for an astonishing fraction of the auction business, even among businesses.

The Traditional English Auction

Auctions evolved in a setting where people could hear and see each other. In an English auction, a would-be purchaser bids a price that is a prescribed increment over the current price. The increment is sometimes called the *tick*, especially in securities markets. Bidding continues until nobody wants to bid higher, and the winner is the last bidder. The seller may set an *initial-bid* price, and may also set a secret *reserve* price. If the final auction price is below the reserve price, no sale occurs. Finally, the seller must determine the length of the period of waiting for the next bid. This period is often called *going, going, gone*, the traditional declaration of an auctioneer that the auction is about to close for want of another bid.

The duration of an auction matters. The designer of an auction sets the initial-bid price, the bid increment, and the length of going, going, gone in order to set the right pace for an auction, not so fast as to prevent buyers from making intelligent decisions, but not so slow as to waste their time. Typical bid increments are around 3 percent of the bid price, so the next bid after $60 would have to be, say, $62. In a

> The duration of an auction matters.

live, in-person auction, going, going, gone lasts only a minute or so, but in Internet auctions, it is usually longer.

As I discussed in the first chapter, an English auction automates dickering. The auction is essentially the same as going to one buyer, saying, "Give me a price"; taking that price to another buyer, saying, "Can you beat this price?"; and continuing cycling among all buyers until nobody is willing to beat the current price. The final buyer pays a price equal to the cutoff price that the runner-up bidder was willing to pay, plus the bid increment. Figure 2-1 illustrates this basic property of the English auction.

English Auctions on the Internet

eBay pioneered the adaptation of the English auction to the Internet. Hundreds of web sites offer auctions in similar formats.

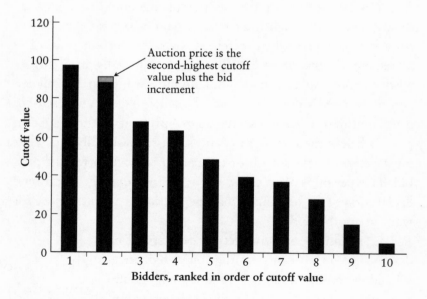

Figure 2-1. The outcome of an English Auction
The bars show the cutoff values of ten bidders, arranged in order. The winner is the bidder on the left with the highest cutoff value. The winning bid is the cutoff value of the bidder with the runner-up cutoff value, plus the bid increment (shown with crosshatches).

The basic challenge that the eBay model solved is that bidders in an Internet auction lasting several days don't want to have to stay tuned to raise their bids. In the eBay model, you do not enter your actual bid—the software does your bidding for you. You specify an upper limit for your bid. eBay calls the process *proxy bidding*. Your bid is shown on the screen to other bidders as the amount you would have bid in person—that is, the previous bid plus the bid increment. An Internet auction proceeds like a live auction, but the bidders don't have to be logged on. Your upper limit is kept completely secret. If somebody enters a new bid above your revealed bid, but below your upper limit, the software raises your revealed bid to the new bid plus the bid increment; you are still shown as the winning bidder. If the new bid is above your upper limit, the new bidder is shown as the current winner and you generally receive an email inviting you to reenter with a new, higher upper limit.

What would happen if the ten bidders shown in figure 2-1 bid in an Internet auction? We need to think about how bidders set their upper limits in order to answer this question. Suppose the bidders enter as their maximum bids the cutoff values shown in the figure. They might reason that they know their own limits, and might as well put the limit in as the maximum price up front (we'll see in a moment that this is not what most people do). In this case, as the bids are entered, the current auction price will be the second-highest maximum bid plus the increment. For example, if Mr. 3, with a maximum bid of $67 is the high bidder, and the next highest is Ms. 6, with a maximum bid of $38, and the increment is $2, the auction price displayed at that point will be $40. Once all the bidders have joined the auction, the auction price will be as shown in figure 2-1, the maximum bid of the runner-up bidder plus the increment.

Notice that timing does not matter in the auction, when people bid their true maximum values at the outset. No matter what the order of the bids or when they come in, the result is the same. In fact, the auction could be run with sealed bids and the result would still be the same. There is no auction excitement or drama when everybody bids true maximum prices.

Does it make sense to enter your true maximum when you first submit a bid to an Internet auction, or should you put in a low bid first and see what happens? If you know your maximum, there is no compelling reason not to enter it as soon as you bid. Remember that your maximum is kept secret in all Internet English auctions. Your maximum really is the same as instructing a robot to keep rebidding so that you are the winning bidder as new bids come in from others, up to your maximum.

When should you place your bid? Under the conditions we have been discussing, where all bidders are eventually going to enter bids with their true maximums, it just does not matter. Whether you bid at the beginning, middle, or end of the auction, or when others bid, has no effect on the outcome. The winner is always the bidder with the highest maximum, and the price is always the runner-up maximum plus the bid increment. Keeping an auction open for a few days rather than collecting all bids at one moment is just a convenience for the bidders.

But if you have joined even one Internet auction, you probably know that what I have just said is a fairy tale. Timing is everything. Experienced users of auctions know that there is a big advantage in being the last bidder. They watch the last minute of an auction, hitting the refresh button every few seconds, poised to hit the submit button for their own bids a few seconds before the auction closes. This crowding into the last few seconds is much stronger in eBay, where auctions have fixed closing times, than in Internet auctions with going, going, gone procedures.

Bidders don't know their cutoff values before an auction begins. Rather than having a good idea of the maximum they are willing to pay, they have a general idea that they want an object, and a firm desire not to pay more than it is worth. They would like to gather information from others—especially experts—about an object's value. And they use auctions for that purpose. When less-informed people see that experts have joined an auction and pushed the price to a certain level, they can be confident that the experts know that the object is worth at least the current auction price and probably more. So it makes sense to wait to see what the experts are doing and then try to outbid them by a bit.

Now think about auction strategy from the point of view of an expert. Once the expert bids, the less-informed bidders will try to outbid the expert. If the expert can bid last, the expert will probably be able to get the object for a lower price. So experts try hard to be the last bidders. When the auction ends at a predetermined moment, they try to place their bids within the last few seconds.

Experts try hard to be the last bidders.

Figure 2-2 illustrates how this works in practice. It is the eBay display for a completed auction for a pair of tickets for the Red Sox–White Sox game of July 23, 2000. The auction opened on July 14 and closed in the evening of July 17. The bid amount col-

User ID	Bid Amount	Date of Bid
doctor.bob (3)	$125.50	Jul-17-00 17:36:37 PDT
samgarfield (61)	$123.00	Jul-17-00 17:48:33 PDT
vikingfour (7)	$110.00	Jul-17-00 17:43:52 PDT
ur2clever (1)	$105.00	Jul-16-00 20:05:01 PDT
riadind (0)	$100.00	Jul-15-00 07:32:18 PDT
wjwi (0)	$75.00	Jul-15-00 07:31:55 PDT
cator5 (0)	$50.00	Jul-15-00 07:31:26 PDT
seth815 (0)	$40.00	Jul-15-00 04:32:50 PDT

Figure 2-2. Bids in a Typical eBay Auction
The auction started in the afternoon of July 14. The early bids were from inexperienced users, at unrealistically low maximum prices. The auction closed at 17:48:48 on July 17. Three experienced users bid in the last five minutes. samgarfield—probably a dealer—placed a bid only 15 seconds before the close. The author, doctor.bob, placed a bid with a maximum price of $150 (a preemptive bid) about 2 minutes before the close. He won at a price of $2.50 above the next-highest bid.

umn shows the maximum bid for all bidders except the winner.
The winner—me—bid $150 but paid the second-highest maximum, $123, plus the bid increment of $2.50. The serious bids all
came in the last 5 minutes. The likely most expert bidder, samgarfield, managed to sneak his bid in only 15 seconds before the
close. He knew that nobody would be able to see his bid, learn
his opinion of the value of the tickets, and enter a new bid.

This example illustrates a central tension of e-market design:
*less-informed players benefit from knowing about the bids of
better-informed players, while the better-informed players lose
from displaying their interest.* Transparency—displaying large
amounts of information during the market process—attracts
some participants and repels others. e-Market design has to balance transparency against other objectives.

Auctions at Amazon have almost the same format as those at
eBay, except that Amazon uses a going, going,
gone process to conclude its auctions. The auction does not close until there have been no bids
for ten minutes. samgarfield would be less likely
to bid in an Amazon auction because, if he
became the leading bidder, the others would have
at least ten minutes to respond. Amazon has
selected much higher transparency than has eBay.

> Transparency
> attracts some
> participants
> and repels
> others.

And Amazon does much less auction volume
than eBay. One factor in eBay's success may be its superior
attraction to experts, who disfavor transparency and prefer to be
able to make last-second secret bids.

Transparency is an issue we will encounter over and over in
this book. In some settings, it is best to be opaque—at Priceline,
discussed in chapter 6, only the buyer and the seller see the price
for their deal. Partial transparency is probably best in some settings; OffRoad Capital tells you the current price in its securities
auctions, but does not disclose individual bids or information
about bidders. The market will determine the best amount of
information to disclose in each e-market setting. Attempts to regulate transparency have often been wrongheaded to date. For

example, the Securities and Exchange Commission compels transparency in transactions in stocks for which trading is established, but prohibits transparency in the auctions that determine the initial trading price of a stock at its IPO. Complete transparency in trading makes it too easy for dealers to find out who is breaking a collusive arrangement among the dealers to worsen the terms under which customers buy and sell stocks. Complete opacity in IPOs prevents bidders from learning about the value of an IPO from the bids of others.

In many e-markets, the collection of bids or offers or orders is called the *book*. For example, people in the stock market speak of the order book. An auction where a bidder can see the bids of earlier bidders is called an open-book auction, as opposed to a closed-book auction with sealed bids. In a semi-open book, bidders know the total volume of bids and the current price, but cannot see the individual bids.

Sealed-Bid Auctions

The Internet English auction replicates a traditional open auction, where bidders can raise their bids as other bids come in. Another auction format is the sealed-bid auction, where bidders cannot see one another's bids. A primary motivation for sealed bidding is to prevent collusion among the bidders. It is much harder to enforce an agreement among bidders to cheat the seller by bidding low, when the conspirators cannot check one another's bids.

In the traditional sealed-bid auction, the winner is the highest bidder and the winner pays the amount she bid. This format is the *first-price sealed-bid* auction. The sale occurs at the first or highest price bid. In a first-price auction, your bid price determines both whether you are a winner and how much you pay. You have an incentive to set a price up toward your cutoff, in order to avoid missing out on an opportunity to buy the item for less than it is worth to you. But, once your bid is in a range where you think it is likely you will be the winner, you will shade your bid price downward in order to avoid paying more. Formulating a bid is more complicated in a first-price auction than in an English auction, and your one bid in a first-price auction will be lower than your final bid in an English auction for the same item with the same bidders.

So, apart from discouraging collusion, which is better for the seller, a sealed-bid first-price auction or an English auction? In the first-price auction, the bidders shade their bids downward, to the disadvantage of the seller. In an English auction, the auction price is the cutoff value of the runner-up rather than the winner, a different disadvantage to the seller. In general, we can't say which effect is larger. Under certain circumstances, economic theory shows that it is an exact tie—the shading-down effect exactly offsets the disadvantage of receiving a price equal to the runner-up value rather than the top value.

One factor favors the first-price sealed-bid auction: in English auctions, the runner-up has an important role—her bid sets the price received by the seller. If the runner-up doesn't bother to take part in the auction, the seller will suffer by receiving a lower price. The seller needs to provide the runner-up an incentive to make a bid. Suppose the runner-up knows that one of the bidders places a higher value on the object than she does. She knows that she will be outbid and does not bother to take part in the auction. In the worst case, all bidders except the one with the highest value don't bother to bid, and the guy with the top value can win with a low bid.

The sealed-bid first-price auction gives the seller the benefit of the participation of the runner-up. The runner-up will reason that there is some chance that the highest-value guy may shade his bid down so much as to give the runner-up a chance at winning. And the highest-value guy will reason that there is some chance of a high bid by the runner-up, and bid high enough to be sure to win in that case. The seller gains, either by selling to the highest-value guy at a good price or by selling to the runner-up at a good price.

On the other hand, the English auction has a benefit to the

seller I discussed earlier—bidders learn about the value of an object by seeing the bids of others. The same people who might bid low in a sealed-bid auction will bid higher with confidence once they see others bidding.

William Vickrey invented another type of auction, the *second-price sealed-bid* auction, often called the Vickrey auction. In this model, the winner pays the runner-up's bid price. Bidders submit their bid prices without seeing rival bids. The winner is the bidder with the highest price. But the winner pays the price bid by the runner-up bidder.

In a second-price auction, your bid price does not determine how much you pay. Rather, it determines only whether you are the winner. Because the price you pay is set by another bid, your bid price makes no difference to the price you pay if you win. In deciding on your bid, there is only one thing to think about— avoiding becoming the winner by paying more than the item is worth to you. Hence you will set your bid price to that cutoff point.

Notice the connection between the second-price auction and the English auction. In both models, the winner is the bidder who places the highest value on the object, but the winner pays a price controlled by the value of the runner-up. There is one difference in detail—in the English auction, the winner may pay the runner-up's value plus the bid increment, whereas in a second-price auction, the winner always pays the runner-up's value.

Why would a seller choose a second-price sealed-bid auction over an English auction or a first-price sealed-bid auction? First, if there is a value to transparency because bidders learn from each other, then the seller will choose an English auction. To attract expert bidders who do not want to share the information conveyed by their bids, the seller may want to choose a closed-book sealed-bid auction model. If participation by the runner-up is not an issue—if bidders are unaware of the values placed by other bidders on the object—then the second-price model may be preferred.

Notice that a second-price sealed-bid auction requires an auctioneer who is independent of the seller and is trusted by the bidders. If the auctioneer lets the seller peek inside the order book and place a bid, the seller can force the price up to the price bid by the winning bidder. All the seller has to do is to place a bid just below the winning bid. That price will become the auction price under the second-price rule. Bidders will not bid their true values unless they really trust the auction organization and believe it is independent of the seller. When the seller runs his own auction, it has to be an English auction or a first-price sealed-bid auction.

eBay—king of Internet auctions—has a model that is close to second-price sealed-bid. There is no better case for the importance of Vickrey's idea. Recall that the important bids in some auctions, such as the one in figure 2-2, all come in at the last minute or second. There isn't time for one bidder to see another bid and respond to it. The other bidder has made sure this won't happen. In effect, the book is closed and the bids are sealed. When eBay processes the bids, its proxy bidding procedure implements essentially Vickrey's rule. It finds the second-highest bid, adds the increment, and declares the highest bidder the winner at that price.

At Amazon—one of eBay's rivals in general Internet auctions—the going, going, gone rule ensures that the book is open and no bids are sealed. There cannot be a last-second bid at Amazon, because the rule calls for ten minutes of no bidding before the auction closes. One of the reasons eBay is so much more successful than Amazon is that eBay was the first successful player in the market and Amazon has always had to try to catch up. Another reason may be that eBay auctions are more attractive to buyers—there is a bigger chance of picking up a valuable object at a low price at eBay than at Amazon. By giving the buyer a better deal and attracting a large community of buyers, eBay may have a more successful overall business model than Amazon. Though sellers would choose Amazon's auction model and eBay's buyer community if they could, because they don't have this choice, they generally choose eBay's auction model to get access to eBay's buyer community.

Transparency after the Auction Ends

Up to this point, I have considered transparency during the auction—how much do bidders know about the interests and valuations of other bidders as bids are placed? e-Market design also needs to consider how much information to publish *after* the auction finishes. Take the example of my bid with a maximum price of $150 for Red Sox tickets. eBay did not publish that number in its display of auction results in figure 2-2. My bid shows as $125.50, the amount I paid, not the $150 I bid. This is fine with me. I would not want ticket dealers to know that doctor.bob was the kind of person who bids high. In some future auction, a dealer might bid in his own auction to try to force my bid up. For example, in figure 2-2, if the seller had entered a bid for $140, I would have had to pay him $142.50.

> e-Market design needs to consider how much information to publish *after* the auction.

TradeOut: Surplus Merchandise

Disposal of merchandise that does not sell through normal channels is a natural area for e-markets. Prices are uncertain, so an auction model may be appropriate. TradeOut.com is making a serious run at developing this market, though its success is hardly assured. TradeOut is a partner of eBay, which is a substantial investor in TradeOut. Meg Whitman, CEO of eBay, sits on Trade-Out's board of directors.

TradeOut offers a wide variety of auction and fixed-price formats to sellers. These include a standard eBay-style auction with second price achieved by proxy bidding, a sealed-bid auction where bidders can set expiration times, a hybrid posted-price offer with bid option, and a pure quoted-price offer with quantity discounts across products.

The last two formats are novel and popular among sellers. In the hybrid format, a seller fills orders immediately at a posted price. A buyer can also submit a bid below the posted price. Such a bid is similar to a limit order in the stock market and is filled the moment the seller reduces the asking price. This format permits the seller to mimic the traditional department store pricing strategy of gradual markdowns until a product sells out. The buyer has the choice between purchasing for sure at the stated price or gambling that the product will not sell out at that price, but will be available later at a lower price.

In the format with a pure quoted price, a seller is usually trying to dispose of many related items—such as over-the-counter drugs—that are likely to appeal to the same purchasers. The purchaser receives a quantity discount for the total purchase from the seller. This e-market model is the subject of chapter 6.

TradeOut has moved substantial volumes of used trucks for the truck leaser Penske and used shipping containers for GE Capital. Volume appears to be low for all of TradeOut's true surplus-merchandise offers. The company may be on the way to specializing in selling off used capital goods for leasing companies.

Auctions for Identical Items

The auctions discussed so far in this chapter are for single objects. Their main use is in secondary markets—individuals trading collectibles and businesses selling off used equipment. When a seller wants to make a deal for hundreds or thousands of newly produced items, one answer is to place them in a lot and then sell the lot in an English auction. But this approach is restrictive, because it means that there can be only one buyer. A higher total sales value usually could be achieved by selling to a number of buyers, in quantities each chooses. A convenient auction procedure exists for this situation.

The process collects bids from purchasers. Each bid specifies a price and a quantity. At the end of the auction, the bids are sorted by price, with the highest price first. Bidders are allocated units in this order until all of the units on sale are accounted for. The last successful bidder will probably get only a fraction of the number desired—a *partial fill*. Either bidders have to agree in advance to accept a partial fill, or the last winning bidder has the option of declining to purchase.

Figure 2-3 shows the results of an auction on eBay for five

User ID	Bid Amount	Quantity	Date of Bid
rl3n (16) ⭐	$40.00	1	Jul-18-00 11:51:16 PDT
pandac99 (6)	$33.00	1	Jul-18-00 11:17:33 PDT
ryantrujillo (7)	$32.00	1	Jul-18-00 11:01:08 PDT
movies3 (8)	$31.00	2	Jul-18-00 06:02:00 PDT
mandt (14) ⭐	$31.00	2	Jul-18-00 10:58:18 PDT
dialtone911 (3)	$30.85	1	Jul-17-00 05:10:37 PDT
copytalk (116) ⭐	$28.77	1	Jul-13-00 06:32:35 PDT
lynnepolk11 (101) ⭐	$28.00	2	Jul-13-00 08:39:08 PDT
tarbud (34) ⭐	$28.00	2	Jul-13-00 13:09:53 PDT
trixie999 (78) ⭐	$24.00	2	Jul-11-00 12:03:53 PDT
cork94305 (5)	$23.50	1	Jul-11-00 07:32:37 PDT
sharif08 (82) ⭐	$22.50	1	Jul-09-00 12:34:12 PDT
catsuptwo (28) ⭐	$21.97	2	Jul-10-00 02:53:56 PDT
atrillion (33) ⭐	$20.01	1	Jul-10-00 00:25:36 PDT
gk8wet (79) ⭐ me	$17.55	1	Jul-09-00 03:13:00 PDT
hkz (71) ⭐	$16.00	1	Jul-09-00 06:02:06 PDT
pond88 (13) ⭐	$15.00	1	Jul-09-00 00:34:36 PDT
a49erfllwr (47) ⭐	$15.00	1	Jul-09-00 07:00:03 PDT

Figure 2-3. Bids for Five Bug Repellers
The bids are in declining order of price, with the time of the bid used to resolve ties (for example, between movies3 and mandt). The top four bidders were the winners, receiving the five repellers.

electronic bug repellers. As in the auctions for single objects, the higher bids tend to come in toward the end, though none of these bidders tried to hit the last few seconds. The bidders down through movies3 were winners; movies3 beat mandt by bidding earlier.

Figure 2-4 shows the bug repeller auction in a supply-and-demand diagram. The horizontal axis is the quantity. The vertical line shows the supply of five units. The downward sloping line shows the number of repellers requested by all the bidders with prices at or above the price shown on the vertical axis. You can think of this line as the demand curve—it shows the number of units that would be ordered at a given price.

The intersection of supply and demand shows the lowest winning bid price. In a standard market setting, this would be the

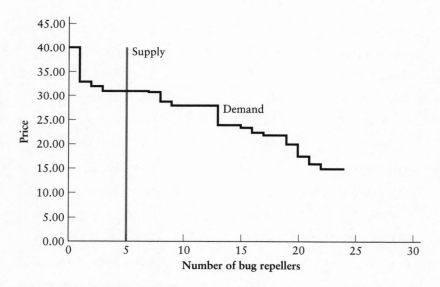

Figure 2-4. Supply and Demand in the Bug Repeller Auction
The demand curve shows the number of bug repellers in the bids, arranged by price. For example, there is one repeller bid at $40 and four at $31. The supply curve shows the five repellers offered by the seller. The auction price and quantity are at the intersection of supply and demand, with a price of $31 and all five units sold.

market price. In the *single-price* version of the multiple-unit auction, all the successful bidders pay the lowest winning bid price, even if they bid a higher price. eBay uses this version, which it calls a *Dutch* auction (Dutch auction means many different things, so I will not use the term). In the auction shown above, all four winners paid the lowest winning price, $31. Auctions for securities—the subject of chapter 3—generally use the single-price format.

Single-price auctions for multiple units are close cousins of the Internet English auction. In both auctions, your bid price does not determine how much you pay. Rather, it determines only whether you are a winner or not. In figure 2-3, as long as ryantrujillo's bid price is above the auction price, he could raise it without having to pay more for his repeller.

The fact that your bid price affects only your participation and not the price you pay means that you can formulate your bid with only one factor in mind—to avoid buying if the price is above your cutoff. You don't have to worry that setting a high maximum price in your bid will cost you more money. Thus the bids submitted to a single-price auction should reflect the full maximum amount bidders are willing to pay.

A second format for a multiple-unit auction has each bidder pay the actual price bid. This is the cousin of the first-price auction for a single unit. Again, bidders will shade their prices downward. What a seller gains from collecting a higher price from the higher bidders the seller may lose from the general tendency to shade bids downward.

Transparency is an issue in the design of multiple-item auctions in much the same way as in single-item auctions. Less knowledgeable buyers will want to see what others have bid in order to figure out what is a good price for items. Experts will bid late to avoid the competition of those who would emulate them. One new factor is present in the multiple-item auction—the rule that ties are resolved in favor of the earlier bidder provides an incentive to bid earlier that somewhat counteracts the incentive to bid late to keep information away from rival bidders.

Another tool used to make auctions more transparent by inducing experts to reveal their bidding interest is the *activity rule*. A typical activity rule bars a bidder from lurking on the sidelines until the last minute. For example, in the OffRoad private-equity auction, you have to bid during the main phase of the auction to have the right to bid in the concluding phase (going, going, gone), when the winners are determined.

> Experts would rather buy in opaque auctions.

Auctions for multiple items can be fully opaque with sealed bids. The auction for newly issued Treasury securities or W. R. Hambrecht's IPO auction are sealed (in the latter case, by the rules of the Securities and Exchange Commission). Again, the choice between opaque and transparent auctions is a close and interesting call—transparency is not an end in itself. Experts would rather buy in opaque auctions.

Buy-Side Auctions

To keep things simple, I have focused on sell-side auctions so far in this chapter. But essentially all the principles of auctions apply to buy-side or procurement auctions as well. Government agencies have used procurement auctions—usually sealed-bid first-price auctions—to place highway contracts, build post offices, and the like. All of the same design issues arise in buy-side auctions. Auctions are also widely used for business procurement, where quotes are solicited from qualified suppliers and the most favorable quote is accepted. If there is no further dickering, the procedure amounts to a first-price sealed-bid auction. If there is dickering until no potential supplier wants to outbid the winner, the procedure amounts to an English auction. Because procurement auctions are only just becoming an important force in corporate procurement, we can expect their design to evolve over the coming years until they reach a stable form. Chapter 4 looks at B-to-B procurement auctions.

Two-Sided Auctions

Auctions for multiple items operated by a neutral organization can permit bidding by both buyers and sellers. Electricity auctions are the leading example of these two-sided auctions. Although two-sided auctions could be a standard feature of neutral B-to-B exchanges for many standardized goods, this model has not become the rule. Rather, in most B-to-B exchanges, each buyer conducts its own auction among the suppliers it has qualified.

> In most B-to-B exchanges, each buyer conducts its own auction.

Imagine a B-to-B exchange for standard Ethernet components. The exchange runs weekly auctions for each kind of component, such as 8-port hubs. Purchasers of hubs enter bids specifying the number desired and the maximum price they will pay. These purchase bids are just like those in the eBay auction for bug repellers. In addition, hub makers enter supply bids specifying quantities available and minimum acceptable prices. After all the bids are in place and the auction is closed, the exchange finds the price by constructing the supply-and-demand diagram shown in figure 2-5. The exchange accepts the bids of all the suppliers who set minimum prices no higher than the auction price. Similarly, it accepts the bids of all customers who set maximum prices no lower than the auction price. With the proper choice of price, the quantity supplied will equal the quantity desired by winning purchase bidders, with the following qualification: either one supply bidder or one purchase bidder may receive a partial fill. This bidder will be borderline, in the sense of having specified a minimum or maximum price that is equal to the auction price.

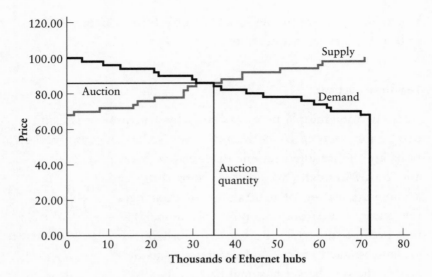

Figure 2-5. A Two-Sided Auction with Both Purchase and Sale Bids
*The demand curve shows the cumulation of purchase bids, as in figure
2.4. The supply curve shows the cumulation of sale bids, the number of
units offered for sale at the price on the vertical axis or at a higher
price. The auction price and auction quantity are found at the intersection of demand and supply.*

A two-sided auction can use the principle of the single price,
or it can charge all the buyers their bid prices and pay all the sellers their bid prices. When all buyers pay the same price, and all
sellers receive that price, the exchange operating the auction does
not make any profit from the auction. The exchange charges participants a transaction fee or an entry fee. On the other hand, an
exchange that charges buyers their actual prices and pays sellers
their actual bid prices will make a profit, since all but the mar-
ginal participants are paying more than the auction price for
their purchases and receiving less than the auction price for their
sales. Players will choose whether to join an exchange on the
basis of this cost, among other factors. In practice, all of the two-
sided auctions I have seen use the single-price principle and earn
their revenue as fees.

What is the difference between running a single auction for all suppliers and purchasers and running multiple auctions, say, one for each purchaser? A single big auction sets one price for everybody. The auction price measures the scarcity value of the product in the auction. With separate auctions, the scarcity value will be different across purchasers. A purchaser whose auction happens to have a high price would benefit by moving some of its business to a lower-price auction. Or a seller who was supplying a low-price auction would gain by shifting some of its supply to a high-price auction.

If separate auctions are somewhat transparent—if they disclose the tentative auction price before they close—the forces of self-interest will generally operate to equate prices and reduce the losses from different prices among auctions. There may be other reasons for purchasers to run their own auctions, such as differences in product specifications or differences in the best time to run the auctions. Consequently, it is not surprising that many exchanges are set up with separate auctions, rather than a single big one.

Auction Abuses

e-Commerce has some obvious dangers. Sellers may lie about what they are selling, or they may fail to deliver after the auction. Buyers may fail to perform. These are not dangers specific to auctions, but rather dangers of doing business at all. I will concentrate on the ways people abuse auctions and distort electronic markets.

Shill Bidding

Dishonest sellers may bid in their own auctions. The motive is to raise the prices that legitimate buyers pay. The practice is called *shill* bidding. In auctions like eBay, where there is little attempt to qualify bidders, a seller can enter a bid just by creating a new

eBay identity. In auctions with serious qualification of participants, including checking business and bank references, it is not
easy for a seller to bid directly, but still easy to enlist a friend to
bid. All participants in all auctions of all kinds should be alert to
the possibility of this abuse. To simplify my discussion, I will consider auctions conducted by
sellers, who want to raise the sale price, but the
same danger exists in buy-side auctions, where
the buyer wants to lower the price.

Participants in
auctions should
be alert to the
abuse of shill
bidding.

In Internet English auctions for single items or
single-price auctions for multiple items, there can
be huge payoffs from an adroit bid by the seller.
Recall that the sale price in an English auction is
the second-highest bid price plus the price increment. The winning bidder pays this amount. If the seller places the right bid,
the seller can become the second-highest bidder, right behind the
winner. Then the winner is forced up from paying just above the
legitimate second bid to the winner's cutoff or maximum price.
This danger has existed in auctions throughout history—live
auctioneers are said to "take bids off the wall" to induce higher
bids from the floor.

In the auction where I bid a maximum price of $150 for Red
Sox tickets, I faced the risk that the seller might guess that I was
bidding high, and force my price up to $150 from the level of
$125.50 that I actually paid. For example, the seller might have
put in a bid with a maximum price of $140, which would have
raised the price I paid to $142.50. Luckily this did not happen.

The downside of bidding in your own auction is that you may
win the auction. Then you lose the opportunity to sell to the
legitimate high bidder, and you owe the auction organization its
fee. A cheating seller has to balance this danger against the benefit of raising the price paid by an outside purchaser.

If the cheating seller can look at the top bidder's maximum
price before the auction closes, then the balance shifts decisively
in favor of cheating. If my baseball ticket seller knew that I had
bid $150, and he were the cheating kind, he would have all gain

and no risk from bidding $149.99. Thus the integrity of the Internet auctioneer is paramount. The whole idea of disclosing your maximum bid to the web site and letting its auction robot raise your bid up to the maximum would be foolish if you thought sellers could peek at that critical piece of information.

I have not heard of any instances of leakages of bid information from web sites to sellers. But it is easy to imagine that buyers would be suspicious of Internet English auctions where the seller

> The integrity of the Internet auctioneer is paramount.

was also the operator of the auction. This is one instance of the question that pervades discussions of e-commerce—will e-commerce markets be operated by neutrals or by organizations of buyers and sellers? Will Covisint, the buying organization owned by the U.S. automakers, be trusted as an auction operator, or will it lose business to a neutral exchange?

What should you do as a bidder if you are worried that your supposedly secret maximum bid may leak to the seller, or that the seller might somehow divine it? Simple. Just enter a low maximum price in your bid, just high enough to make you the winner. Stay tuned at the close of the auction, and raise your bid just as you would in a live auction.

Many bidders in Internet English auctions behave this way, raising their bids as the auction progresses, rather than entering a single bid with a well-chosen maximum price. One reason may be that they aren't completely sure that their maximum price is secret.

The dangers of bidding by cheating sellers are even greater in some cases where multiple items are sold. Figure 2-6 offers an example. There are bidders willing to pay more than $130 per unit, but not quite enough interest to drive the price to that level. To get enough demand to sell all 40,000 units, the price has to be $83. If the seller puts in a bid for 1,000 units with a maximum price of at least $131, the auction price will be $131. The extra price applied to 39,000 units is about $1.9 million. Hard for the seller to resist!

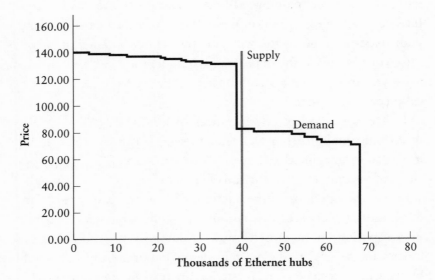

Figure 2-6. This Auction Is Vulnerable to Cheating by the Seller
If the seller bids for 1,000 units at a price of $131, the auction price will jump to $131 from $83, which will raise the seller's revenue by about $1.9 million.

The example shows the danger of a fully transparent single-price auction. Securities auctions are generally completely opaque (Tokyo, U.S. Treasury, Hambrecht IPOs) or only partly transparent (OffRoad Capital). But eBay's single-price auctions for multiple items are fully transparent—all winning bids are shown during the auction. In principle, bidders should avoid bidding at values much above the current auction price, in order to avoid giving the seller the incentive to enter the auction if a situation develops along the lines of figure 2-6.

Revising or Retracting Bids

Auctions need to have strictly enforced rules about revising bids during the auction, including rules against the retracting of bids. The appropriate rules are that purchase bidders cannot lower their maximum prices or reduce their quantities and that sale bidders cannot raise their minimum prices or reduce their quantities. Otherwise, abuses will tempt the players.

If a buyer can retract a bid or make it less generous, then an appealing strategy will be to deter other bidders during the auction by placing large bids with high maximum prices early in the auction. This will cause other prospective bidders to stay out of the auction. Then, at the last minute, the buyer can change the bid to one with a low maximum price and obtain the product at low expenditure.

The corresponding strategy for a supplier is to enter a large supply bid with a low minimum price, to deter bids from other suppliers. Then the bid is revised at the last minute to specify a high price.

Vandalism

Auctions attract vandals—bidders who use untraceable identities to place phony bids and ruin auctions. When the Playstation 2 first hit the market, hundreds of eBay auctions sprouted, placed by sellers who hoped to make a quick profit from the shortage in stores. The market price was about double the list price. In some of the auctions, bids of $15,000 appeared. These vandal bids harmed both the seller—who had to start the auction over—and the highest bidder. Recall that eBay keeps the maximum price of the highest bidder secret, not only during the auction, but afterwards. When a vandal bids a meaningless high price, everyone can see the maximum price of the previous high bidder. The vandal seriously compromises one of the most important features of the eBay auction model, the secrecy of the maximum price of the high bidder.

> The only protection against vandalism is a system for qualifying bidders.

The only protection against vandalism is a system for qualifying bidders by requiring them to submit credentials. In auctions for stocks and bonds, bidders provide extensive personal information that is verified through phone calls and credit reports. Fortunately, most eBay auctions do not attract vandals. It's probably no coincidence that auctions for video games—devices that appeal to young teenage boys—are most likely to receive vandal bids.

Illicit Communication between Sellers and Bidders

Sellers may communicate with bidders outside the auction process. Many times this is constructive—for example, the bidder might want to know more about the product on sale. But the communication can also abuse the auction process. For instance, in baseball ticket auctions (not the one shown in figure 2-2), I have received emails from sellers offering to terminate their auctions and sell to me on the side, at a price higher than the one showing. The motivation is to avoid part of the auction fee.

The Winner's Curse and Auction Enthusiasm

Many people worry that the price in a sell-side auction will come out too high, or in a buy-side auction, too low. Two lines of thought back up this worry. First, there is a concept in economics called the *winner's curse*. Second, people are concerned that they will be caught up in the auction process and be carried away, bidding higher prices than make sense the next day.

At the heart of the idea of the winner's curse is the property of auctions developed in the first chapter as well as this one: the person who places the highest value on an object will be the winner in an auction for it. This property is all to the good if the values are correct. But suppose that bidders make mistakes in their evaluations. Then there will be a tendency for the winner to be the person who overstated the value of the object the most. The winner's curse is the excess price that results from the valuation errors.

The U.S. government runs auctions for oil-drilling rights on federal lands. Oil companies run geological tests to evaluate the oil in the ground. These tests are imperfect, so it is likely that the high bidder will be a company whose test showed the largest amount of oil. The winner will overpay for the drilling rights if it is not careful.

The winner's curse cannot be a universal feature of auctions. If it were, everybody would want to sell in auctions and nobody would want to buy. Bidders with a good grasp of auctions—whether from experience and intuition or from studying auction theory—shade their bids to offset the winner's curse on the average. Building contractors know that they have a better chance of landing a contract if they mistakenly bid too low. They put in a factor that adjusts all their bids upward to take account of the tendency. It remains true that they will make mistakes and get a disproportionate share of their business from cases where they underestimate costs, but they won't operate at a loss.

> Bidders shade their bids to avoid the winner's curse.

One way of seeing that the winner's curse is not a widespread feature of Internet auctions is that the winners are often the most experienced participants. Many savvy dealers buy inventory from Internet auctions. They are the least likely to suffer from the winner's curse, but they are outbidding the less experienced who are potentially subject to it.

Marketing research on new auction models has shown that many people have concerns about their self-control in auctions. They fear that they will be carried away by auction excitement and pay more for an object than they would in a calmer setting. They fear winding up in the shoes of the bidder who paid $200,000 for Jackie Kennedy's fake pearls. These people may be comforted by an auction that moves slowly, where each bid can be made deliberately. e-Market auctions tend to be more leisurely than traditional English auctions, because the participants do not have to gather in one place.

Dominance of an e-Market

Figure 2-7 shows a rough measure of market shares among consumer auction sites. eBay accounts for 60 percent of all auction listings. The next-biggest player, Yahoo, has only 28 percent. Amazon and the sum of several dozen other auction sites each amount to 6 percent of the market. The shares here are listings. eBay's share of actual auction volume and revenue is much higher, because its auctions attract more bidders and because many rivals, including Yahoo, did not charge for their basic auction services when these numbers were collected.

Why is it so hard to compete against eBay? A successful auction site delivers millions of potential bidders to its sellers, and millions of auctions to its buyers. It's a meeting place, popular because it is easy to meet the right people there. A rival has a gigantic chicken-and-egg problem. To attract sellers' auctions, it has to deliver bidders, but to attract bidders, it has to have auctions. Among eBay's rivals, only Yahoo has come close to solving this problem. eBay has over five million auction listings and Yahoo over two million. No other site has cracked a million. The FairMarkets auction site, offered jointly by the powerful partnership of Microsoft, Lycos, and Excite, has fewer than 200,000 listings.

Yahoo has not achieved a viable auction business, because it does not charge for basic auctions (you can pay for enhance-

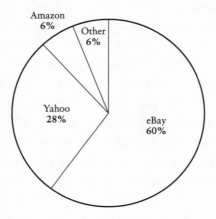

Figure 2-7. eBay Dominates the Online Auction Business

eBay accounts for 60 percent of Internet auction listings, according to data from AuctionWatch. Yahoo accounts for most of the rest. Other general-purpose auction sites including Amazon, and special-purpose sites such as MusicHotBid list a small fraction of total online auctions.

ments). Sellers and bidders flock to eBay despite the price advantage at Yahoo.

eBay exploits a *network effect* to maintain its dominance of consumer auction e-markets. When a business's customers form an interactive community, a network effect is likely to be a factor. Much of Microsoft's dominance of desktop software comes from network effects. It's hard to get customers to switch to another word processor when people trade files in Microsoft Word and when they can consult other Word users when they encounter problems.

In most cases, the company that dominates a market because of a network effect is the first to the market, as eBay was. Sometimes there is a race that starts out roughly even, as there was between the VHS and Beta videotape standards. When network effects are strong, as they are in videotapes, one seller will become dominant. Thus Beta disappeared from the market. Network dominance is powerful. The 8-millimeter videotape, introduced after VHS owned the market, is more convenient and economical, and is technically the equal of VHS. But it has made no headway against VHS, which will remain the videotape standard until the technically far superior DVD displaces tape completely.

> Where network effects are strong, one seller will become dominant.

Dealers

Many e-markets attract dealers, people who make a profit from trading. A dealer operates on both sides of a market. Dealers thrive if they can buy low and sell high on the average. They typically hold inventories of the products they buy and sell—that is, they buy before they sell. But some dealers go short, selling before they buy.

eBay provides a fascinating glimpse into this process, because it is so big and discloses so much information. On the one hand, eBay provides coin collectors with an alternative source to traditional coin stores for building their collections. In that respect, eBay has probably taken business away from coin dealers. But eBay has also opened up a huge source of supply for dealers. You can see this in any eBay coin auction, because many of the bidders are dealers. They troll eBay auctions for coins available at good prices. Many of the losing bidders are dealers who put in a slightly low bid in the hope of picking up a bargain.

In addition to traditional dealers building stocks from eBay auctions, eBay has created a community of pure eBay coin dealers who buy and sell only on eBay. They have the same role that Nasdaq dealers have in the stock market—making money by selling at higher prices than they buy for. Whereas Nasdaq dealers are serious, full-time professionals, pure eBay dealers often do their trading as a sideline.

The eBay coin market has four kinds of players: (1) coin collectors who generally are on the buy side, building collections, (2) people liquidating coin collections, who are just on the sell side, (3) coin shop owners who are on the buy side, building inventories to sell in their shops, and (4) pure eBay dealers, equally active on the buy and the sell sides.

Here is the result of a typical eBay coin auction, for an 1881 silver dollar:

User ID	Bid Amount	Date of Bid
dp1408 (109)	$207.50	Sep-12-00 17:24:43 PDT
kfrm65 (17)	$205.00	Sep-12-00 15:06:45 PDT
buzzer.com (238)	$202.00	Sep-09-00 09:25:30 PDT
windstallion (118)	$192.50	Sep-05-00 20:57:37 PDT
dkrempco (40)	$160.00	Sep-06-00 06:31:57 PDT
55lobster (299)	$155.00	Sep-05-00 19:33:48 PDT
davescoinstore (16)	$115.00	Sep-03-00 18:31:16 PDT
eliascomaro (143)	$101.55	Sep-03-00 8:27:54 PDT
pnavey (27)	$95.00	Sep-03-00 00:13:22 PDT
coins5 (474)	$39.55	Sep-03-00 04:04:19 PDT

The parentheses show the number of people who have put in feedback about doing business with each bidder.

The activities of dealers on eBay make it a B-to-B exchange even for items like coins. Many transactions for collectibles on eBay go from one dealer to another.

Will B-to-B e-markets change the role of dealers? Will e-Steel or MetalSite be more efficient at supplying the small steel user than the existing steel dealers who hold inventory in warehouses? Only time will tell. The creation of an e-market gives customers another solution to the problem solved earlier by a dealer. But e-markets also create opportunities for dealers. At a time when steel girders are quoted on an e-market at a low price, a dealer can buy, with the plan of meeting customers' needs later. Or the dealer might decide to sell the girders on the same e-market later when the price is high.

Dealers are rarely involved in core supply-chain procurement by large producers. But smaller producers often buy from dealers. In the market for computer memory chips, small computer makers go to dealers if they can't arrange supplies directly from chip makers. In the steel business, dealers buy from steelmakers when they spot a good deal and then resell to small steel customers such as construction contractors. Dealers are particularly active in markets for used equipment or surplus or distressed merchandise.

A contest between e-markets and dealers is going on in Nasdaq, the main subject of chapter 5. Pure e-markets, where investors trade directly with each other, are growing. The biggest and oldest is Instinet, but others, such as Island and Archipelago, are on the move. But the dealers will not disappear from Nasdaq. There will always be a role for a nimble mind guessing when stocks are cheap on the e-market and when they are expensive.

The Offer-Bid-Accept Auction

Another auction model is common in emerging e-markets: *offer-bid-accept*. This model resembles an electronic version of the market for houses. Traders—usually sellers—post asking prices. Buyers make offers, and sellers make counteroffers. One side or the other accepts an offer or a counteroffer, and the deal is made.

Here are some offers pending at ChemConnect World Chemical Exchange:

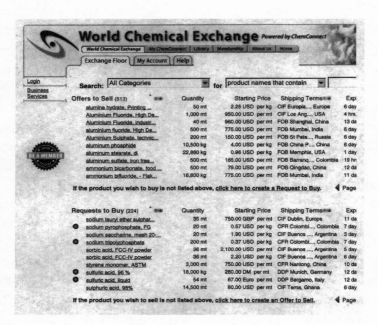

A customer locates a sale offer of potential interest with an asking price of $210 and offers $206 per ton against, which the seller counters with $208 per ton:

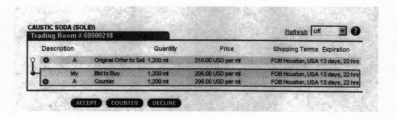

The buyer finds this acceptable and pushes the Accept button.

The offer-bid-accept model is a flexible auction. If there are several bidders, they will keep bidding the price up until all but one of them drop out. During the time when bids are flowing in and rising, the seller will not accept any of them. Once the flow stops, if the seller accepts the current bid of the one remaining buyer, the process is the same as a regular auction, which winds up selling the item to the buyer with the highest value, at a price just above the drop-out price of the buyer with the second-highest value. If the seller continues to dicker with the dropout, the seller has a chance of getting a better price.

The seller's decision about accepting an offer below the current asking price depends on just what the seller might be able to coax out of the current bidder, but also on what other bidders might come along in the next week or two.

eBay lets sellers run a type of offer-bid-accept auction. If the seller chooses, eBay will display a button that a buyer can press to gain the object immediately, at a price the seller specifies. If nobody presses the button, the normal eBay auction rules apply.

The request for quotation, or RFQ, is a standard tool of traditional business—a document that initiates negotiations with suppliers. The resulting informal auction is called *RFQ and negotiation*. It is most frequently used on the buy side, though the logic would apply to the sell side too. A purchaser sends an RFQ to a list of qualified suppliers. They respond with bids. If the model calls for the purchaser to accept the lowest bid, the model is a sealed-bid auction. The sealed-bid auction could use the second-price principle. But in almost all functioning procurement e-markets, the winning supplier receives the price that he bids. As was noted earlier, the first-price rule is mandatory if the seller operates the auction rather than a third party trusted by the bidders.

In the RFQ model, it is common to have additional rounds, where bidders who lost in the first round can have a chance to get the business by rebidding at lower prices. If the purchaser lets this process proceed to its natural conclusion, where no losing seller is willing to make a lower bid in order the get the business, the RFQ process becomes an English auction. The winner will be the supplier with the lowest cutoff price, and the purchaser will pay the cutoff price of the supplier with the runner-up cutoff price.

T A K E A W A Y S

- **The standard English auction provides a neat solution to the problem of getting players to reveal their best prices.** As bidders raise the prices they bid, they come closer to their best prices. The auction ends when the price goes past the best price of all but the winner.

- **Bidders learn from one another's bids if the auction has an open book.** The seller may choose an open book to try to stimulate interest. But expert bidders will prefer a closed book, or they will bid at the very end of an open-book auction, because they give away more information than they receive.

- **The single-price auction offers an effective way to sell multiple identical items.** After bids from many bidders are collected, the items are allocated to the bidders at or above the auction price. That price is chosen so that all of the items on auction are allocated. This kind of auction succeeds in inducing bidders to bid up to their best prices.

- **Auctions are vulnerable to manipulation through shill bidding by sellers.** If the seller can see the auction book during the auction, the seller will be able to spot opportunities to make fake bids to raise the price and force legitimate bidders to pay more. Auctions need to be designed not to reveal this kind of information to sellers.

- **It is imperative that bidders not be permitted to retract bids.** A retractable bid is a perfect tool for finding out the best prices of other bidders or for discouraging others from participating in an auction.

- **Intelligent bidders know how to offset the winner's curse.** A careless bidder may let a valuation mistake become the basis for an excessively high bid—the winner's curse describes the general tendency for the winner to pay too much. But a thoughtful bidder will shade bids downward to adjust for this danger. The winner's curse is only a danger, not an inevitable feature of auctions.

- **An exchange can implement the equivalent of an auction by supporting the offer-bid-accept model.** By soliciting new offers from interested purchasers until nobody is willing to top the current offer, the user of the exchange can run what amounts to an English auction.

3

Auctions for Stocks
and Bonds

S tocks and bonds are natural candidates for auctions. Millions of identical shares trade for each corporation in the stock market, and bonds are generally issued in large numbers of identical units. New stocks and bonds are sold in one-sided auctions. Existing stocks are beginning to be traded in two-sided auctions to compete with traditional stock exchanges. Some experts on stock markets believe that auctions will have a larger role in the U.S. stock market in the future, as the rules limiting them relax further.

For many years, the Treasury of the United States has conducted auctions to place new bills, notes, and bonds in the hands of the public. These successful auctions have accumulated large amounts of experience with auction principles. Auctions have spread to municipal bonds and are beginning to extend to corporate bonds.

Auctions are not a significant part of trade in the U.S. stock market today. But auctions are beginning to be important in markets for private equity—stocks of unregistered companies not eligible for trading in U.S. exchanges. A new investment bank sets the prices of IPOs by auction. And one entrepreneur is running auctions in many publicly traded stocks in competition with the existing stock market.

Treasury Auctions

Every week, the U.S. Treasury holds auctions whose size would make any would-be e-market CEO seriously envious. The Treasury sells billions of dollars worth of bills, notes, and bonds to bidders. Purchasers in these auctions are dealers, banks, and individual investors. The Treasury uses a single-price, multiple-unit auction, in structure just like the one for bug repellers discussed in the preceding chapter. But the scale is stupendous.

On September 18, 2000, the Treasury offered $14 billion worth of three-month bills to investors. The owner of one of these bills receives $1,000 on December 21, 2000. The bills sell at auction for about 1.5 percent less than they eventually are worth—the difference is the reward that the owner earns, equivalent to interest. These bills grease the financial system of the United States and the world. They are the most liquid way for investors to hold funds temporarily. Treasury bills are completely electronic, nothing but entries in a computer database maintained with great care by the Treasury.

The auction attracted $32 billion in bids. Each bid specifies a number of bills and a price. The auction is sealed-bid—nothing is disclosed about the bids until after they are all received and the auction is closed. But bidders have a good idea about the likely price, because similar auctions are held every few days, and the bills trade in a secondary market continuously.

The tick in this Treasury auction is $.025, or one four-hundredth of a percent of the $1,000 that a bill is worth when it matures. This is probably the thinnest tick in any auction anywhere. Compare it with the tick of around 2 or 3 percent in the typical eBay-style auction on the Internet. The thin tick reflects the precise information that investors have about the price of the bill and the prices of other ways of parking money with complete safety.

When the auction closes, the Treasury, just like eBay, puts the bids in order of price and fills bids by declining price until it has allocated the entire issue. Absent an amazing coincidence, there will be more bidders at the lowest winning price than there are bills left to allocate to them. In many auctions, the winners are those who bid first. But the Treasury prorates the remaining bills among the lowest-price winning bidders. All receive a fraction of the number of bills they have requested.

> The thin tick reflects the precise information that investors have about the price of the Treasury bill.

All bidders pay the winning price—it is a single-price auction. In 1998, the Treasury—run by a secretary with a Ph.D. in economics—gave in to decades of heckling by economists and switched to the one-price auction method. Traditionally, bidders paid the price they bid. As a practical matter, there is almost no difference between the two auction methods when applied to bills.

Because everybody knows beforehand almost exactly what a bill is worth, the bids are close to each other. Really close. The lowest winning bid, and therefore the auction price, was $984.925. The median among all the winning bids was $984.950, only one tick above the winning price. Some 95 percent of all the winners bid below $985.025, four ticks above the winning price. Although the Treasury does not publish anything about losing bids, it is reasonable to surmise that almost all the losers were low by only a tick or two—less than a dime out of $1,000.

The Treasury accepts noncompetitive bids in its auctions. These bidders agree to buy a specified number of bills at the market price, whatever it turns out to be. Of the total of $14 billion of bills sold in the September 18 auction, $6.5 billion went to competitive bidders and the remaining $7.5 billion to noncompetitive bids from individuals and government agencies. Only in an auction with such a high level of certainty about the auction price would such a large number of investors be willing to take bills or other securities at the market price, no matter what it is. In effect, the noncompetitive bidders reduce the supply to the auction. The competitive bidders faced a supply of only $6.5 billion. The price would have been a bit lower if there had not been so much demand from the noncompetitive side.

Many customers in e-markets want to buy, but they don't want to have to think about the price. They just want to pay the market price. Many securities e-markets have provisions for purchases at the market price. In some cases, such as the Treasury bill auction, the market-price buyers affect the price. In others, such as the stock market auction discussed at the end of this chapter, these buyers have no effect.

> Many customers in e-markets want to buy at the market price.

The Treasury auctions are the most liquid in the world. Nowhere else is the tick so small and the distribution of bids so tight. Auctions for other kinds of securities operate with much more uncertainty.

Municipal Bonds

MuniAuction runs an e-market in newly issued municipal bonds. Several times a month, the company conducts Internet auctions for packages of bonds issued by cities and states. The auctions typically raise $10 million to $100 million. Most of the auctions are first-price, single-item auctions. The winning bidder pays the price it bids and buys the entire bond issue. The bidders are major financial institutions with massive retail capabilities.

Each auction lasts 30 minutes. There is no going, going, gone period. The seller can decide what information to disclose during the auction. When bids are disclosed, however, the bidders hang back until the last seconds, just as in eBay. As a result, the auctions are effectively sealed-bid auctions even if they are not designed that way. It appears that sealed-bid is the preferred auction mode for municipal bonds, since it would be easy for Muni-Auction to add going, going, gone to its auction model to make the disclosure of bids meaningful.

Bidders at MuniAuction have a hand in designing the packages of bonds they are purchasing. The package contains bonds maturing in each of the next 25 years, typically. The city issuing the bond specifies how much money it wants to raise from each of the 25 bonds. The bidder specifies the interest to be paid on each bond.

The winning bid is the one that raises the specified amount of money at least cost to the issuing city. Defining least cost is a bit tricky. All bidders back-load the interest—they propose higher interest rates for the bonds that pay off later. But some back-load more aggressively than others. MuniAuction has a measure called Total Interest Cost (TIC) that captures the aggregate interest burden on the city. The winning bid has the lowest TIC.

On September 20, 2000, the state of Oregon raised about $34 million through MuniAuction. The bids were as follows:

Bidder	TIC	Bid time
Piper Jaffray, Inc	5.3758%	11:57:53 am
Salomon Smith Barney	5.3786%	11:59:00 am
Merrill Lynch	5.3989%	11:59:47 am
Prudential Securities	5.4060%	11:54:33 am
Legg Mason Wood Walker, Inc.	5.4282%	11:59:07 am
Bear, Stearns & Co. Inc.	5.4284%	11:59:29 am
Dain Rauscher Incorporated	5.4393%	11:56:59 am
Morgan Stanley Dean Witter	5.4748%	11:57:32 am

Notice that all of the bids came in the last six minutes and four of them in the last minute. The daredevils at Merrill Lynch snuck in only 13 seconds before the auction closed. They were taking no chances that other bidders would learn from their bid.

The e-market for Oregon bonds is not as liquid as the one for Treasury bills. The bids for Treasury bills tended to differ by $.025 out of $1,000, which translates into one one-hundredth of a percentage point in the interest rate that the bidder earns. Here the difference between the best and worst bids is a full tenth of a percentage point. And all of the bidders are serious players in the bond market, with access to detailed information about the prices of other similar bonds.

MuniAuction's e-markets for municipal bonds actually account for a tiny volume of the hundreds of billions of dollars worth of securities that the company auctions every year. Most of the volume comes from sales made by infrastructure clients, such as giant FreddieMac, the quasi-federal mortgage bank with hundreds of billions of dollars of assets. MuniAuction provides the software and expertise for these clients to run their own bond auctions.

Corporate Bonds

e-Markets for corporate bonds are just getting organized. The veteran investment banker W. R. Hambrecht operates one called OpenBook with some interesting features. In broad design, it is the same as Treasury auctions: a single-price auction for multiple items. OpenBook successfully sold $300 million in bonds for Dow Chemical on August 15, 2000.

Bids in the OpenBook auction are not prices; rather, each is a rule for determining a price. Hambrecht designates a benchmark Treasury bond when it sets the auction up. Bids specify prices in relation to the actual price of the Treasury bond when the sale closes. This feature means that fluctuations in the overall bond market don't cause the auction price to depart from the market price later when the deal closes. Specifically, a bid states a spread in the return that the bond owner will receive, stated as an interest rate. The spread in the Dow Chemical auction was 1.01 percentage points—the winners paid a price for their bonds that gave them an interest rate 1.01 percentage points above the similar Treasury bond that served as the benchmark. All bidders who proposed a spread below 1.01 percentage points were winners—they were bidding, in effect, a price above the auction price.

The OpenBook auction has a novel going, going, gone rule. In the first hour, investors make initial bids. The volumes of initial bids are shown in a display on the OpenBook web site. Each bid receives a time stamp, which determines who receives bonds among those who wind up bidding exactly the auction price.

The open-book phase of the Hambrecht auction provides feedback to bidders about the value of the bonds. When the interest shown in the first phase is strong, bidders know that they will have to bid higher to win the bonds they want. Those who bid early are providing a service to other bidders and to the seller. They are compensated by the priority they earn with earlier time stamps.

During the second hour, you submit your final bid. This bid is not shown to other bidders; the book is closed after the first hour. You can raise your price (lower your spread) by a certain amount without sacrificing your time stamp. If you exceed the threshold (0.04 percentage points or 4 basis points in the Dow auction), you get a newer, less advantageous time stamp. After the second hour elapses, the auction closes by the standard rules for single-price auctions.

Closing the book helps thwart collusion among bidders.

Closing the book in the second phase of the Hambrecht bond auction helps thwart collusion among the bidders. Because the same purchasers—big funds and bond retailers—are likely to be bidders in one auction after another, the danger of practices that limit the vigor of bidding is particularly great. When the actual bids that determine who wins the auction are kept secret, it is much more difficult for these practices to develop. Sealed bids are a traditional feature of government procurement auctions for just this reason.

OpenBook accepts noncompetitive bids or market bids in the same way as the Treasury auction.

The OffRoad e-Market for Private Equity

OffRoad Capital is a startup with a growing business raising equity funds for development-stage companies. These companies have more than business plans and founders; they have employees and customers and revenue. Most have received venture funding at earlier stages. But they are not yet ready for IPOs and subsequent trading in the stock market. Historically, firms at this stage have raised more capital from venture (at high cost) or sold equity through investment banks, which place the equity with pension funds, other institutions, and wealthy investors. There is no organized market for trading private equity. Investors generally hold the stocks until the company goes public (30 percent of companies), is acquired (30 percent), or goes under (30 percent). A few companies (10 percent) remain independent and private for many years after startup, but the great majority put marketable public shares in the hands of investors through an IPO, return cash to investors through a buyout, or go out of business with a complete loss to investors.

OffRoad is a new kind of investment bank with an Internet business model. Companies seeking to raise new equity post extensive descriptions of themselves on OffRoad's web site. These offering documents are in a standard format developed by OffRoad. They include extensive analysis of financial data. One of the ideas of the OffRoad model is to bring the standardized disclosure and documentation of the public stock market to the market for private equity. Another is to encourage discussion among investors in email discussion forums that are limited to credentialed members of the OffRoad investment community.

OffRoad sells private equity in a semi-open-book single-price auction. The rules of the auction encourage early bidding by well-informed investors so that their bids become part of the information considered by other bidders. The type of information about the order book available to bidders is chosen to prevent manipulation by bidders or by issuers.

Investors using the OffRoad system place orders (auction bids) that specify the maximum price per share they are willing to pay and the total number of dollars they want to invest. In every other securities auction, buyers specify the number of shares they want, so the total amount they pay is not known until the auction price is determined. In the OffRoad system, investors know in advance how many dollars they will be putting into a deal if their bids are successful. The number of shares they receive is determined after the end of the auction as the dollar investment divided by the auction price. In other words, investing through OffRoad is like investing a certain number of dollars in a mutual fund, rather than buying a certain number of shares and finding out later how much they will cost.

One of the customs of investment banking is to structure deals to achieve traditional levels of prices. For private equity, the standard share price is $3 to $5, while in IPOs it is around $12. The bankers split the shares of their issuers as needed to hit these prices. So if an OffRoad issuer has existing shares that are worth around $15 apiece, OffRoad will set the deal up with a 3-for-1 split, in order to get a price around $5 per share. Then, during the auction, the bid increment, or tick, is usually $0.25. Bid prices have to be $3 or $3.75 or some other multiple of $0.25— you can't bid $3.17.

An offering on the OffRoad system has three key parameters— an offering price, a minimum number of shares, and a maximum number of shares. You can't enter a bid for a price below the offering price. The deal will fall through if the minimum number of shares cannot be sold. If investors place orders for more total dollars of investment than the offering price times the maximum number of shares, OffRoad uses a single-price auction to find the price and allocate the shares among the investors.

OffRoad's process for selling a new issue of private equity has three phases. The first is a period of a week or so when investors may examine the documents posted by the company issuing the stock, watch a streaming video of the company's principals, participate in a discussion forum with other investors about the deal, and place nonbinding orders. During this phase, OffRoad displays the offering price and the minimum number of shares to be sold. If there is ultimately not enough interest to sell the minimum number of shares at the offering price, the offering is canceled and no investor actually buys any shares. The first phase ends when total orders received surpass the minimum, or when the deal is canceled for lack of investor interest.

The second phase is the auction itself. Orders from this point on are strictly binding. During this phase, investors can track the progress of the auction at OffRoad's web site, where they can see the current auction price and the price they need to bid in order to enter the deal. Sometimes the second price is higher, because earlier bidders receive priority, and there are enough of them that a new bidder has to move to a higher price to get in ahead of them despite their time priority.

Each time a new bid arrives, the OffRoad auction engine recalculates the auction price and determines how many shares each investor would receive if the auction concluded without any more bids. Figures 3-1 through 3-3 illustrate how this works.

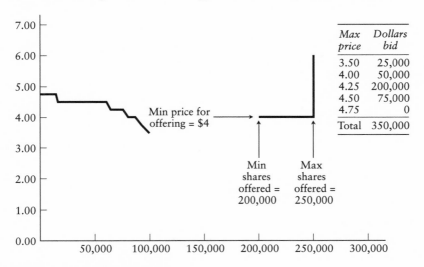

Figure 3-1. Early in the OffRoad Auction
The bids, shown in a table on the right and by the downward-sloping line on the left, fall short of the minimum specified. If the auction closed at this point, the deal would be called off and no shares be sold.

The table on the right of figure 3-1 shows the bids that came in early, totaling $350,000. The downward-sloping line in the graph shows the bids as a demand curve for shares. When price falls to one of the tick points, say, $4.50, all of the investors who bid $4.50 as their maximum price get added to demand, which accounts for the flat parts of the line at each tick price. As you look at prices declining between ticks, you can see that the number of shares demanded rises, because the number of dollars is the same but the dollars buy more shares at lower prices.

If the auction ended with only the orders in figure 3-1, the deal would be canceled, because there was not enough interest to sell the minimum number of shares at the minimum price. On the other hand, figure 3-2 shows the auction with enough additional orders that the deal would go through, even without more orders. If the auction ended with these orders, the price would be the minimum, $4 per share. Not every order would be filled.

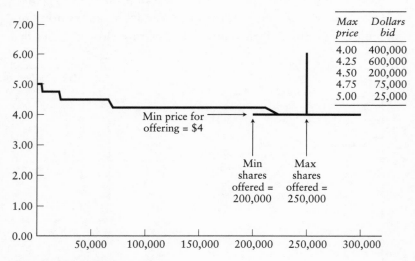

Figure 3-2. Later in the OffRoad Auction

More bids have come in. The total number of dollars bid, $1.3 million, is enough to fill the deal at the minimum price of $4, but there are not enough bids with maximum prices above $4 to lift the auction price above $4. If the auction were closed at this point, the auction price would be $4. All bids with prices over that level would be filled, and bids at $4 would be filled in starting with the earliest bid, until the maximum was reached.

OffRoad uses price priority first, and then time priority—earlier bids are the first to be filled. All orders with maximum prices above $4 are filled completely. Then enough of the bids with maximum prices at $4 are filled, in the order that they came in, until all the shares in the offering have been allocated. As chapter 2 noted, in an auction for multiple items like shares, one bidder is likely to receive a partial fill. In the OffRoad system, this is the bidder who placed the last winning bid with a maximum price that turned out to be the same as the deal price determined in the auction.

> In an auction for multiple items like shares, one bidder is likely to receive a partial fill.

Figure 3-3 describes the auction after enough orders have been placed to push the auction price above the minimum specified for the deal. Now all the bidders with maximum prices of $4, the minimum, are out of the deal. They don't show on the demand curve in figure 3-3, because they have been pushed off to the right. To be in the deal, an investor must bid at least $4.25, and only the earlier bidders at that price would get

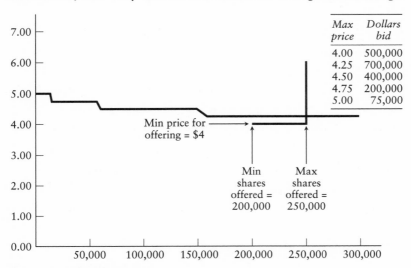

Max price	Dollars bid
4.00	500,000
4.25	700,000
4.50	400,000
4.75	200,000
5.00	75,000

Min price for offering = $4

Min shares offered = 200,000

Max shares offered = 250,000

Figure 3-3. The OffRoad Auction Ends
Even more bids have come in. The dollars bid by those with maximum prices of $4.25 or higher are sufficient to account for the maximum number of shares available at a price of $4.25. All bids with prices over $4.25 are filled, and those at $4.25 are filled in order of time priority.

into the deal. An investor consulting the OffRoad web site at this point would learn that the current auction price was $4.25, but that the bid price necessary to get into the deal would be $4.50.

As new orders come in and the auction price rises, orders with maximum prices below the new auction price are bumped out of the deal. The OffRoad system automatically sends these investors emails to see if they want to reenter the auction by raising their maximum prices. Orders with maximum prices equal to the auction price may also be bumped if they were not entered early enough. As bumped investors raise their maximum prices, the auction price may rise more.

When the offering enters the auction phase, OffRoad announces a day about a week later when the offering will enter the closing phase. To prevent investors from waiting until the last minute—as happens so often in eBay auctions—OffRoad uses the principle of going, going, gone in the last phase of its private equity auctions. The auction does not end until several hours have passed without any change in the auction—no price change and no change in the allocation of shares to investors. No bidder can sneak in at the last minute.

Another rule of the final phase is that no new dollars can come into the auction. Investors must decide how much they want to invest by the end of the middle phase. They can raise their maximum prices only in the final phase. The effect of the final phase is to find out which investors really want the shares by showing their willingness to pay higher prices. Those with lower willingness are bumped out.

OffRoad encourages an issuer to make the minimum price a true walk-away price, not what the issuer believes is the true value of its shares. This is a key difference between the OffRoad system and standard investment banking, where the offering price is chosen in advance and is the price the issuer receives even if there is more than expected interest among investors in the offering. In the OffRoad model—and in the Hambrecht model to be discussed next—the issuer benefits from a higher price if investors like the offering.

OffRoad's experience since its first offering in June 1999 has shown that the market design achieved its basic goals. Orders tend to come in smoothly during the two weeks or so that most offerings are open. Investors who are not sure about the value of a deal have a chance to see other investors commit money at a visible price. In this respect the degree of transparency seems to be helpful to investors. On the other hand, all of the details of the order book are kept secret. Issuers never have an opportunity to bid in their own auctions to take advantage of situations like the one we saw in the last chapter where a small bid can drive up the price. The only information that issuers and investors know is the total number of dollars in all orders, the current auction price, and the price that would be required to get into the deal with a new order. No auction abuses have occurred.

OffRoad has applied for a business method patent that covers many aspects of its business model. Chapter 8 discusses the controversies over this kind of patent.

W. R. Hambrecht's IPO Auction

Traditionally, investment banks have taken companies public according to a standard formula. When a company has reached the point where its size and value merit continuous public trading of its stock, the company picks an investment bank to handle the offering. IPOs have two purposes. In most cases, the more important of the two is the inauguration of public trading. The second is the selling of new shares to raise additional funds.

The Securities and Exchange Commission (SEC) regulates public trading with a heavy hand. An important function of an investment bank, along with the lawyers, is to satisfy the SEC's exacting requirements for documents supporting an IPO. The SEC imposes restrictions on the process that limit the role of e-markets. The silliest is that the SEC has to approve the offering price of an IPO, even though the price will be determined in an open market from the time of the IPO onward. Because of the requirement of price approval, IPOs cannot be sold in partly transparent auctions like the OffRoad offering process (OffRoad cannot take itself public on its own system, for example). The traditional approach to pricing is for the investment bank to gather a tentative book of orders, decide upon a price, work with the SEC to get the price approved, and then sell the shares at that price to the bank's customers.

An auction could formalize this process by building the order book electronically through an Internet auction. Because of the SEC's silly rule, there can be no disclosure of the tentative auction price during the auction—it would be completely opaque.

William Hambrecht conducts IPOs in exactly this fashion in a business called OpenIPO. He runs a single-price sealed-bid auction for IPO shares. Hambrecht does not promise that the IPO price will be the auction price according to the principles of the preceding chapter. Rather, he promises that the price will not be any higher than the auction price and, if a lower IPO price is chosen, that all winning bidders with maximum prices at or above the chosen price will receive shares. At a lower price, there will be more winning bidders than shares available. To deal with this problem, Hambrecht allocates to all the winners the same proportion of the shares they bid for.

The system has functioned according to plan. The Hambrecht auction finds prices that are close to the prices that occur in later trading. Traditional investment banking generates large discrepancies in both directions. Sometimes a stock embarrasses the investment bank by trading at prices well below the offering price. More frequently, especially in hot markets like that in 1999, trading starts above the offering price, a situation called a *pop*. When there is a substantial pop, the issuing company has left money on the table—it could have received more money for the shares it sold in the offering. With a pop, the issuing company is giving an instant capital gain to the investors who buy at the offering price. If pops occurred routinely—which they don't—it would make more sense for a company to issue no stock when it went public and then to sell stock at the market price later.

As in many areas of e-commerce, there is much more to the economics of IPOs than just the amount of money passing from the issuing firm to the investors in the case of a pop. Investment banks have long-term relationships with investors—who are mainly financial institutions—and with issuers. Changing the benefit that the investors get from IPOs by pricing them closer to the market will alter all of these relationships. The success of the Hambrecht IPO model turns on Hambrecht's success in retaining effective relationships in the setting without the value from pops to spread around.

> When trading starts above the offering price, the issuing company has left money on the table.

One value of a pop is publicity. A company going public at $12 per share and trading immediately at $28 gets attention in the financial press that may be more effective promotion than millions of dollars of advertising. To put it the other way around, Hambrecht's IPOs, which never have pops worthy of news coverage, have been criticized in the press as boring or even unsuccessful for lack of a pop. Presumably one of the reasons that Hambrecht reserves the right to set an offering price below the auction price is to generate a pop for its publicity value.

The immediate financial value of the pop goes to the investors who buy shares directly from the investment bank. They can turn around and sell the shares for an instant capital gain as soon as trading begins—and they often do. But the investment bank gains because the bank alone decides who gets shares. A bank will allocate large numbers of shares to institutions that will bring other lucrative business to the investment bank, such as trading other stocks.

Auctions for Traded Stocks

It's common to talk about the stock market as a continuous "auction." But it's not really an auction. Suppose you wanted to sell a significant number of shares, say, 50,000, in Dell Computer. If you just told a broker to sell them for the best possible price, you would probably be disappointed with the results; your price would turn out to be below what most people were paying around the time you sold. Turning the sale over to a broker is no different from telling a real estate broker to sell your house without your being involved in considering the offers and picking the best one. You can't expect a broker to act in your own interest. A professional trader desiring to sell 50,000 shares would set up an informal auction by calling around and finding the best deal. But a retail investor buying or selling a significant block of stock cannot count on a broker to do the same thing.

> You can't
> expect a broker
> to act in your
> own interest.

The stock market can do a fine job for professionals who run their own informal auctions and a fine job for retail customers who want to buy and sell a few hundred shares. The next chapter will look at the details of the non-auction e-market for stocks. But that e-market ill suits the outsider who wants to sell a large amount of stock. I say sell because the main victims of the defects in the stock market are people who were in on the ground floor in successful new companies and want to cash out shares they received as founders or from stock options.

An interesting infant e-market, the Arizona Stock Exchange, or AZX, hopes to correct the problem of the outsider with a large desired trade. The basic idea is to use an e-market to give the outsider the same mechanism for getting a good price that the professional insiders use—offering a trade to the highest bidder. The investor does not call around to gather offers, however; rather, his trading intention becomes a bid in a computer auction. Professional traders in the stock respond to the bid to sell by placing bids to buy.

AZX runs two auctions a day in a collection of stocks where the benefits of its auction model are likely to be greatest. These are tech stocks like Red Hat, Qualcomm, Dell, and Cisco. The auctions use the single-price multiple-unit model, similar to the

OffRoad model (Steve Wunsch, the founder of AZX, was a consultant in the OffRoad auction design). They take place at 9:29 A.M., just before Nasdaq trading begins, and 5:00 P.M., an hour after Nasdaq closes. Here is an illustration of the bids that might be found in an auction for Dell Computer:

Price	Purchase bids	Cumulative purchase bids	Sale bids	Cumulative sale bids
38½	33,000	33,000		109,000
38¼	8,000	41,000	7,000	109,000
38⅛	8,000	49,000	50,000	102,000
38	12,000	61,000	10,000	52,000
37⅞	23,000	84,000	34,000	42,000
37¾	26,000	110,000	6,000	8,000
37½		110,000	2,000	2,000

The shaded row shows the auction outcome. All shares change hands at $38. The purchasers bidding that price or above (who want a total of 61,000 shares) have a chance of receiving shares. All the sellers offering that price or below (who want to sell a total of 52,000 shares) have a chance of selling. Because the selling volume is below the buying volume, all of the sellers actually sell their desired amounts. Some of the buyers come up empty. The AZX rule—different from that of most auctions—is that orders are filled in the sequence they came in, regardless of price, provided they specify prices at least as good as the auction price. So the buyers who don't get the 9,000 shares they were hoping for may be those who bid prices above $38. This rule encourages early bidding.

You might think that an investor placing a bid at 9:00 A.M. faces a risk in choosing a price half an hour before the auction closes. Information might come along that made the bid price obsolete. It is not unusual for the prices of stocks like Dell to change by 5 or 10 percent in half an hour of Nasdaq trading. But the risk is minimal. Suppose you say that you are willing to buy Dell at $40 a share, but some bad news comes out and the price is actually $38. You don't pay $40, you pay $38. The worst that can happen is that you buy the shares at $38 when you might have chosen not to buy at all after hearing the bad news. The single-price principle is a powerful way to avoid serious mistakes.

> The single-price principle is a powerful way to avoid serious mistakes.

Recall that many investors don't want to bid a price, but instead want to accept the market price. AZX has a special kind of market-order bid to help these investors. These bids do not enter the auction. After the price is determined, two things happen. First, all the market orders to buy are matched with market orders to sell. These become transactions at the auction price. Second, any leftover shares from the auction are matched with the remaining market-order shares. For example, the 9,000 shares of unfilled purchase bids from the example given earlier could be used to fill up to 9,000 shares in sell market orders. There is no guarantee that a market order will be filled.

TAKEAWAYS

- **Treasury auctions prove the efficiency of the single-price auction model for securities.** The Treasury sells tens of billions of dollars worth of securities every week in an e-market.

- **MuniAuction moves huge volumes of bonds by auction, using what is in practice a sealed-bid model.** MuniAuction does not have a going, going, gone procedure, so expert bidders submit their bids in the last few seconds. Because other bidders cannot respond, these are effectively sealed bids.

- **OffRoad Capital uses an auction model for private equity with a partially open book and going, going, gone.** In the OffRoad e-market, bidders can see the current auction price during the auction, but not individual bids.

- **Hambrecht's IPO auction model solves some of the problems of IPOs, but is limited by SEC regulations.** The auction has a strictly closed book. It has helped companies go public without leaving money on the table, because the auction price is usually close to the market price on Nasdaq once public trading starts.

- **Auctions may move into listed securities, but so far the one player, AZX, has not generated much volume.** Although a periodic auction in listed stocks would help investors with large trades avoid the danger of front-running, AZX has not persuaded enough investors to create adequate volume on its auction exchange.

4

B-to-B Procurement Auctions

The U.S. economy delivers about $10 trillion worth of goods and services each year to final users— consumers, capital-goods customers, and foreign customers. The components of these products change hands several times before finished goods reach final customers. One company mines raw materials, another makes components, a third assembles components, and a fourth markets the product to customers. Three B-to-B transactions before delivery to users is probably close to average. The grand total of B-to-B commerce is easily $30 trillion per year in the United States alone, and close to $100 trillion in the world.

Every B-to-B transaction involves a deal. Dickering is the rule in relations among businesses. e-Markets will thrive in B-to-B commerce to the extent that they can improve deal making by automating dickering. e-Markets using formal or informal auctions are gaining rapidly because they provide the natural solution to the dickering problem. Real-time deal engines are also gaining in B-to-B commerce, generally for products previously ordered over the phone from paper catalogs.

Procurement at Eveready

Eveready manufactures all kinds of batteries, including lithium AA batteries used mainly in cameras and flash units. The company buys hundreds of thousands of products from thousands of suppliers. Some of these products make their way into batteries. These are direct purchases in the supply chain. Some are commodities, such as chemicals or metal, and others are highly technical components, such as the membrane that surrounds the chemicals and the circuit breaker that is built into every lithium battery. Other purchases are indirect or what is called MRO (maintenance, repair, and operations). These include office supplies, floor wax, and all kinds of other stuff. The third category is plant and equipment.

Many supply-chain purchases are critical for product safety and quality. For Eveready's lithium batteries, the circuit breaker falls into that category. Because the batteries can put out a huge amount of power, they can cause fires in cameras and flash units if there is a short circuit. A few dangerous fires in the early days of lithium batteries convinced the industry that each battery needed its own circuit breaker. In Eveready's battery, there is a disk just under the top of the cylinder that blocks an excess flow of current that might start a fire.

Although the disk costs only around a nickel, it is a critical component. Eveready spends about a year studying a proposal from a new circuit-breaker supplier before ordering the new part in quantity. Eveready does extensive lab tests on samples and builds test batteries containing the new devices. It also studies a new supplier's reputation to be assured that the supplier can perform consistently at production quantities. If a new supplier passes all the tests and can beat the price of the existing supplier, Eveready will begin phasing in the new part in its battery production. The two companies will write a long-term supply contract with many detailed clauses.

Eveready buys specialized machinery for its battery operations from capital-goods suppliers, many in Europe or Japan. Machines are typically made to order. There are only a few qualified suppliers of many of the machines. Again, the process of specifying and ordering capital equipment is time-consuming and detailed. It results in a detailed supply contract.

Eveready's supply-chain requirements for lithium batteries include a number of standard industrial commodities, such as the lithium that gives the batteries their name. The company buys the commodities from numerous qualified suppliers. Prices in these commodity markets fluctuate substantially, and Eveready switches suppliers fairly frequently.

e-Markets will not invade the supply chain for technical products.

Eveready buys thousands of MRO products, mostly similar to those bought by other manufacturers. These products tend to have stable prices, and there is relatively little switching among suppliers. In many cases, people at Eveready order the products from catalogs.

Eveready and other manufacturers are using the Internet more and more aggressively to improve the efficiency of purchasing. All of the transactions I just described are being moved to the Internet at least in some respects. e-Commerce is advancing rapidly for the supply chain and for MRO. But the e-markets are taking over at different rates for different kinds of purchasing.

For mission-critical technical parts and equipment, such as the circuit breaker, there is little role for an e-market. The relationship between Eveready and its circuit-breaker supplier is complicated and durable. It's like a marriage. A large amount of effort goes into setting up the relationship in the first place, and the effort continues as long as the relationship lasts. It would be inconceivable for Eveready to put out an RFQ, study the resulting bids, and pick a circuit-breaker supplier. It takes a year or more to determine if the supplier has a part that performs in the field.

As a general matter, e-markets will not invade the supply chain for technical products where performance is hard to assure. Another factor operating against e-markets is cooperation between buyer and seller in the design of a component or piece of equipment. An RFQ-bid process standardized in an e-market is unlikely to support large amounts of cooperative design work. Custom-made capital equipment will probably continue to be purchased through ongoing negotiations where price and design are worked out over weeks or months of time. An e-market can't contribute much to those negotiations.

e-Markets are more fully developed for MRO products.

Supply-chain commodities and low-tech components are quite another matter. e-Markets are growing rapidly for products that can be fully specified in an RFQ or in a seller's offering materials. Some type of auction format works well for these inputs. There are active independent e-markets doing substantial volumes of business in industrial chemicals, metals, and cattle. Captive e-markets handle hundreds of billions of dollars worth of procurement of injection molded plastic components, metal fabrications, commercial machinings, printed circuit boards, fasteners, corrugated packaging, and other noncritical components and inputs.

e-Markets are even more fully developed for MRO products. Because prices are more predictable and less volatile, the posted-price e-market works well. MRO web sites resemble consumer e-commerce sites like Amazon. Purchasers order products from catalogs with posted prices. Companies often receive blanket discounts or rebates off the posted prices. In some cases, each customer company has its own set of negotiated prices. Posted-price e-markets are the subject of chapter 6.

FreeMarkets

FreeMarkets is the largest player in online industrial procurement. The company, founded at the dawn of the Internet era in

1995, had the good fortune to grow to the point of going public before the B-to-B market crash. FreeMarkets' business model has kept it growing at a time of disappointment for neutral B-to-B exchanges. The company supports the captive procurement operations of large companies, such as United Technologies, Quaker Oats, Owens Corning, and Eaton. Products handled through its service include injection molded plastic parts, commercial machinings, metal fabrications, chemicals, printed circuit boards, corrugated packaging, and coal. These low-tech components and industrial commodities suit trading in procurement e-markets. They do not include critical components with significant cooperative development.

FreeMarkets is anything but a dot.com. You can't log on to its site and check out what's available. Rather, the company is a combination of a consulting business and an applications service provider. FreeMarkets calls its customers "clients." In setting up a new e-market procurement function for a client, FreeMarkets starts by identifying potential suppliers and qualifying them for the product. The company believes it has a substantial efficiency advantage over its clients in this step and can open up a client's pool of potential suppliers to many more than with traditional procurement.

The second step in FreeMarkets' work with a client is to write a detailed, complete RFQ. An important improvement in efficiency in its approach is to put everything into the RFQ rather than spend time separately with each potential supplier, explaining verbally what the client is trying to buy. In this respect, FreeMarkets is persuading its clients to adopt the Japanese approach to RFQs, which are famously thorough. The RFQ places the desired procurement into lots—for example, in the procurement of cardboard cartons for Owens Corning, the requirements of each plant for the coming two years make up one lot. Although all qualified suppliers may bid on all lots, suppliers may choose to bid on selected lots, such as those closest to their own production facilities.

The first two steps are essentially consulting activities.

FreeMarkets bills them at monthly rates of something like $30,000 per project. The next step is to run a set of procurement auctions. Like most B-to-B and other high-value auctions, these are open for quite short periods—typically 10 or 20 minutes for each lot. The standard FreeMarkets auction has an open book; each bidder can see the bids, but not the identities, of its rivals. The going, going, gone rule requires a period of one minute to elapse after the last bid; each bid after the designated 10 or 20 minutes extends the period for another minute.

Figure 4-1 shows data for one lot in an actual FreeMarkets auction for plastic car parts. The client had most recently paid $745,000 for these parts in this quantity. Bidding began at $738,000 and descended to $585,000 during the designated 20 minutes of bidding. The auction required 13 one-minute overtime bidding periods to complete going, going, gone. The final price was $518,000.

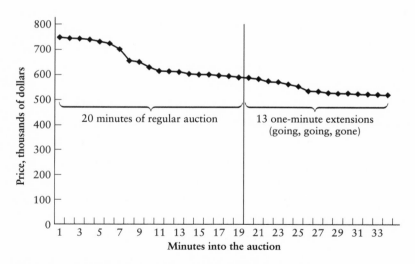

Figure 4-1. FreeMarkets Procurement Auction for Plastic Moldings
The price starts with the first bid at $738,000. As the bids pour in, the price declines as the suppliers compete with each other for the business. After the designated 20 minutes have elapsed, bids are still coming in, so the auction enters overtime periods of one minute each. Finally, in the 13th overtime, the bidding stops and the final price is $518,000.

The FreeMarkets auction—like Hambrecht's IPO auction—has only an advisory role for the client. Bidders know that the lowest bid will not necessarily win, because the client will consider dimensions apart from price. Quality and delivery performance are important factors in the final decision.

FreeMarkets generates a rough measure of its value added by comparing the auction price to the price most recently paid for the same items. These savings have averaged about 20 percent and summed to about $2 billion on more than $10 billion in auction volume.

FreeMarkets is a business with a well-developed revenue model. Most revenue comes from fees charged for setting up procurement e-markets, independent of the results. Some revenue comes from incentive provisions based on savings or volume. Revenue is about $14,000 per auction lot. But expenses are much more. Exclusive of R&D cost, FreeMarkets spends about $20,000 per auction. As the company continues to scale up, analysts expect it to become profitable. FreeMarkets' market capitalization is about $1.5 billion.

> FreeMarkets is a business with a well-developed revenue model.

As the limited potential role for neutral B-to-B exchanges has become more apparent, the wisdom of FreeMarkets' business model has become apparent as well. Large companies want to run their own procurement operations, and FreeMarkets' consulting-ASP business model fits that desire. Still, many questions hang over FreeMarkets. The company's clients learn a lot by working with the FreeMarkets consultants. The clients have the alternative of developing internal expertise and purchasing auction services from any number of ASPs that offer them, such as EDS's eBreviate. Or the clients could host their own auctions, using widely available auction software such as Moai's LiveExchange. After General Electric terminated its relationship with FreeMarkets, a GE executive boasted that summer interns had built procurement auction software for a total budget of $30,000.

FreeMarkets' challenge is the following: e-market procurement services are just another procurement issue themselves. A client could use FreeMarkets' platform to seek bids to replace FreeMarkets' services! FreeMarkets has to hope that these services do not become a commodity whose price is depressed to rock-bottom levels by the same devices that the company has placed in the hands of its clients.

The Next Step in B-to-B Procurement: Perfect.com

FreeMarkets uses expensive human beings to set up each auction. The FreeMarkets model relegates software to the simple task of running the auction. A startup in the same space—Perfect.com—is much more ambitious. Perfect provides software called PerfectMarket to handle the jobs of FreeMarkets' consultants. Perfect sells PerfectMarket as an applications service provider from its own secure servers.

In PerfectMarket, suppliers of all products file detailed descriptions of their capabilities. A company placing its procurement function in an e-market with Perfect's help develops a description of its requirements as an RFQ. PerfectMarket matches buyers with suppliers.

Another important capability of PerfectMarket is the indicative bid. Indicative bids reveal an interest in trading without making a binding commitment. They play the role of the early telephone call in traditional procurement.

A novel capability of PerfectMarket is the virtual auction. In place of FreeMarkets' 20 minutes of excitement in real time, PerfectMarket asks suppliers to formulate bidding rules showing how they would respond to developments during an auction. These rules substantially generalize the simple proxy bid at eBay that automates rebidding up to a specified maximum price. With the bidding rules in place, the company developing a procurement strategy can run auctions several times to refine the strategy. Each auction takes a fraction of a second of computer time.

PerfectMarket's model requires a trusted third party. No supplier will show its bidding rule to a purchaser any more than an eBay bidder wants the maximum price to reach the seller. Perfect wants to stay in the picture as the third party. In that respect, Perfect is positioning itself as more than just a consultant and service provider to purchasing departments.

PerfectMarket is the only B-to-B auction system that supports simultaneous auctions in closely related products. The leading practical example of this problem is radio spectrum auctions run by the government. Many auctions run at the same time for similar spectrum in different cities. A bidder may want to bid for a package rather than for individual cities, because it makes sense to launch a new wireless telephone service only if a block of cities can be served. In these auctions, the seller examines every possible combination of the package bids to find the combination across all auctions that brings in the most revenue. These combinatorial auctions may be useful in procurement because suppliers may not want to supply at all unless they can cover their fixed costs by supplying a package of locations or a package of products.

PerfectMarket is also the only auction system to harness the second-price Vickrey principle in procurement auctions where bids include more than just price. If bidders specify quality, delivery time, and warranty terms, PerfectMarket applies a scoring system to the bids and awards the business to the highest-scoring bidder, but at a price reflecting the second-best score. As in other Vickrey auctions, this principle induces the most favorable bids from participants.

Perfect's initial customers are independent B-to-B exchanges. Unless the current trend against neutrals reverses and they begin to generate significant business volume, Perfect will need to seek business from the purchasing departments of large companies or from their purchasing consortiums. The big news for Perfect would be landing Covisint, e2Open, Petrocosm, or other industry-sponsored exchanges.

Looking After Your Suppliers

Sponsors of e-markets in the supply chain need to recognize that an e-market can be too effective in the short run. An auction can induce suppliers to accept prices that cover the costs of production but not overhead. In the longer run, suppliers cannot remain in business if their prices are that low. Traditional management of the supply chain uses restraint in dickering with suppliers, recognizing that it is possible to get a lower price in the short run at the expense of losing the supplier in the longer run.

> An e-market can be too effective in the short run.

The large savings—20 percent and higher—reported by companies switching from traditional to online auction procurement are almost certainly above what is feasible in the long run. Part of the savings comes from pushing prices down into a range that is too low to keep suppliers in business. Companies achieving spectacular savings at the beginning of one procurement cycle may find prices much higher in the next cycle, because some bidders drop out of what has become an unprofitable line. Eventually the process will reach its zero-profit, zero-loss equilibrium.

Dealers

Many B-to-B markets attract dealers. Dealers are rarely involved in core supply-chain procurement by large producers; Eveready does not buy its circuit breakers for lithium batteries from any dealers. But smaller producers often buy from dealers. In the market for computer memory chips, small computer makers go to dealers if they can't arrange supplies directly from chip makers. In the steel business, dealers buy from steelmakers when they spot a good deal and then resell to small steel customers such as construction contractors. Dealers are particularly active in markets for used equipment or surplus or distressed merchandise.

Will B-to-B e-markets change the role of dealers? Will e-Steel or MetalSite be more efficient at supplying the small steel user than the existing steel dealers who hold inventory in warehouses? Only time will tell. The creation of an e-market gives customers another solution to the problem solved earlier by a dealer. But e-markets also create opportunities for dealers. At a time when steel girders are quoted on an e-market at a low price, a dealer can buy, with the plan of meeting customers' needs later. Or the dealer might decide to sell the girders on the same e-market later when the price is high.

TAKEAWAYS

- **B-to-B procurement e-markets are flourishing in two rather different models: procurement auctions and sales of indirect MRO products from online catalogs at posted prices.** Currently both e-market models manage many billions of dollars of e-commerce.

- **Procurement e-markets handle only part of the supply chain—less technical products easily described by written specifications.** For technical, mission-critical supply-chain inputs, purchasers rely on long-term relationships where price is only one of many complex factors.

- **FreeMarkets, the most successful operator of procurement e-markets, uses a straightforward online open-book auction.** Price rises during the hour or so of the auction. Bidding continues until a minute elapses without a bid. The e-market uses a reverse English auction.

- **Procurement through e-markets runs the danger of pushing suppliers too hard.** In the short run, the adoption of a procurement auction model may push suppliers down to prices close to their variable costs. In that case, they will not be able to cover their fixed costs and may shut down.

5

Exchanges

Sell-side and buy-side auctions and two-sided auctions are excellent deal engines in many settings. They replace dickering effectively when bidders are willing to wait until the next auction closes. But in other markets, the players want immediacy. They want to transact on their own schedules. Their desired e-market operates in real time. The Nasdaq stock market is the leading example of an exchange that meets the needs of this kind of player.

The Nasdaq electronic exchange was the first big electronic market. It is a real-time deal engine, not an auction. There is no automated dickering in Nasdaq. Its design resembles some B-to-B exchanges currently in development—some traders post quotes, and others study the quotes to find the best one. There is a huge amount to learn from Nasdaq.

> Nasdaq is a real-time deal engine, not an auction.

In real-time markets, traders post offers to buy or sell. Prospective customers search the offers to find a suitable one, or prospective suppliers search offers to buy. In Nasdaq, you can post an offer to buy or sell or accept an offer to buy or sell, but within its system, you cannot dicker. In order to dicker, you must call on the phone, and even this sort of dickering is available only to large institutional customers.

A fully articulated real-time exchange shows screens of trading interests to qualified exchange members. The members make two kinds of postings: (1) firm offers to buy or sell stated quantities at stated prices, and (2) requests for quotations stating quantities desired and soliciting offers. Members can respond to these postings by accepting offers, making offers in response to RFQs, or responding to offers with counteroffers to initiate private dickering.

The simplest posted-offer exchange—such as Amazon—contains only offers to sell at stated prices. You can't dangle your own offer in front of Amazon, and you can't dicker. Chapter 1 identified the problem that inhibits e-commerce in the Amazon model—customers will not see the best prices in a setting where sellers make the same offer to everybody. In markets for nonstandardized products or those costing more than $100, customers will avoid an exchange where they can't dicker, in favor of the old business method of calling around on the phone, where they can dicker. Or they will buy in an e-market where a deal engine provides automated dickering.

In the next step up from the Amazon model, you still can't dicker, but you can make your own offer. This is the Nasdaq model. It does not support automated dickering, but it does give traders another tool besides shopping among posted prices. Exchanges using the Nasdaq model flourish in settings where the principle of concealing your best price can be overcome by some combination of forces other than dickering. A fascinating battle is raging in securities markets between the decentralized Nasdaq structure, the centralized approach of the New York Stock Exchange, and new mechanisms that give customers more tools to get the best prices, generally by posting their own offers on electronic systems like Instinet and Archipelago. So far, automated dickering in the form of auctions for listed securities has not broken out in the United States beyond the limited activities of AZX. There is a lot of dickering for large trades in the stock market, but it occurs over the phone the old-fashioned way.

Nasdaq

Nasdaq is the oldest electronic deal engine and still by far the biggest in the world. Every day, over a billion shares of stock trade on Nasdaq's electronic trading system. Nasdaq is an electronic system linking numerous players: market makers, broker/dealers, and the new electronic exchanges known as electronic communications networks, or ECNs. Market makers take on the obligation to trade certain stocks in exchange for the highest level of access to the Nasdaq system. Broker/dealers manage relationships with investors, who are generally not professional traders. The ECNs serve large pension and mutual funds and a growing number of other investors (the ECNs are exchanges in the sense the term is used in e-markets generally, though they are not officially stock exchanges).

The core of Nasdaq is an electronic system for displaying offers to trade.

Nasdaq permits only the first category of offers I described above; there is no way to put out an RFQ on the Nasdaq network: you can make a firm offer to sell a specified number of shares at a specified price, or a firm offer to buy. Although anybody can post an offer on Nasdaq, there are key players who post offers continuously for groups of stocks. These are the Nasdaq market makers, numbering about 550. Each "makes a market"—that is, posts offers to buy and sell at all times—in somewhere from dozens to thousands of stocks. Every Nasdaq-listed company has at least three dealers, and larger companies have dozens.

The core of Nasdaq is an electronic system for displaying offers to trade. All players—investors, professional traders, and dealers—can peruse the existing offers and accept one of them. That is, you can shop for the best deal among all the existing offers to trade in a particular stock. Each offer has two dimensions—the price and the number of shares. If you find a combination you like, you send a message to accept the offer. In most cases, you can accept some rather than all of the shares in an offer, in which case the offer remains on the system reduced by the number of shares you took.

Many different kinds of businesses display trading offers to you and convey your acceptance message to the seller or buyer who posted the offer you are accepting—online and traditional brokers and ECNs. Nasdaq members, including market makers, use Nasdaq's own communications network to accept offers. Large players, such as pension and mutual funds, often deal directly with market makers rather than by means of brokers. They are also huge users of ECNs. The largest ECN, Instinet, got its name from serving these institutions, which for some years were its only customers.

Any player can post an offer to buy or sell instead of accepting an existing one. The same electronic networks will send your offer to the central Nasdaq display system if it is the best offer in their network. In the stock market, an offer from an outside customer is called a *limit order*—an offer to buy or sell a stated number of shares at a stated price.

Nasdaq does not have a centralized system for showing all currently available offers. The system as recently upgraded shows up to three offers to buy and three offers to sell from each market maker or ECN. The offers are the best ones in terms of price—highest buy price or lowest sell price—even if they are for only 100 shares. Market makers and ECNs hold many other offers at less favorable prices. There is no single display of *all* the pending offers. In particular, there is no way to peruse all offers for trading large numbers of shares. Most will be invisible because offers to trade small numbers of shares at slightly better prices obscure them. The invisibility of many of the most important offers is widely thought to be a defect of Nasdaq, but there is no agreement about how to change the situation. Nasdaq could extend its system to display some or all of the offers held by Nasdaq dealers and the ECNs, but the dealers who run Nasdaq are reluctant to give their rivals, the ECNs, so much access to customers.

The biggest collection of offers appears at the largest ECN, Instinet. Here, big pension funds and mutual funds post offers for thousands of shares at a time. On Instinet you cannot see all the offers residing anywhere in Nasdaq, but you can see a good fraction; up to 25 percent of the volume of trades on Nasdaq occurs on Instinet, and for some stocks the Instinet share is much higher than 25 percent.

Figure 5-1 shows how deals are made to trade shares on a

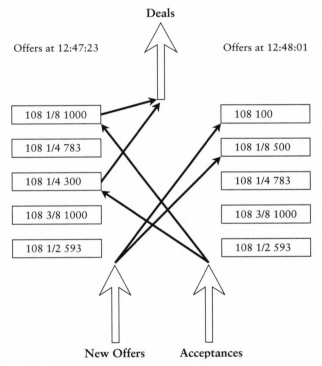

Figure 5-1. The Archipelago Deal Engine at Work
The left column shows the five best offers to sell Yahoo in the Archipel-ago system on September 22, 2000, at 12:47:23 EDT. Each one speci-fies a price and a number of shares. The right column shows the five best offers 38 seconds later. Other players accepted two of the offers by sending messages to Archipelago to turn them into deals (trades). Two new offers came in and were put at the top of the list because they spec-ified better (lower) sale prices.

Nasdaq ECN. The figure shows sell offers for Yahoo stock on the Archipelago ECN at two moments 38 seconds apart. There are two inflows to the system—new offers and acceptances of existing offers. The new offers come from Archipelago's own customers and those of two other allied ECNs. The acceptances come from anywhere in Nasdaq, because the best offer on the Archipelago appears on the Nasdaq screen (known as the *montage*) seen by all Nasdaq players.

It's dazzling to watch the offers arrive and depart on Archipelago's real-time Java display at its web site.

Deals occur in Nasdaq the moment a player sends a message accepting an offer. Needless to say, there is an elaborate system to record the deal and to move the shares from the account of the seller to the account of the buyer. As in any e-market, this follow-up (called "clearing" in the securities business) must be bulletproof in order for the system to attract and retain customers.

What about transactions with dealers? They fit this paradigm as well. Market makers post offers on the Nasdaq system. When you buy shares from a dealer, you are accepting the dealer's offer. Most retail customers are unaware of the mechanics, because they buy through a broker, who then sends the message through the Nasdaq system to make the deal for you.

You might expect that your broker would scan all the quotes to find the best price for your purchase or sale of shares. But that rarely happens. Instead, your broker sends it to the market maker it uses regularly, regardless of the market maker's offer. Big brokers own their own market makers—Schwab, for example, owns one of the largest market makers. You are not cheated by this practice. No matter what Schwab's market maker's current offer, your purchase through Schwab will occur at the lowest offered price on all of Nasdaq. More on the economics of this practice later.

Investors in Nasdaq stocks have to choose their methods of trading in two dimensions. First, you have to decide whether to use a broker, who will almost always use the practice I just described, or to use an ECN. Second, you have to decide whether to accept an offer posted in Nasdaq or to post your own offer. For purchases of a few hundred shares, it hardly makes any difference. If you are thinking of accepting an offer, you might as well use a broker, because the broker will arrange for you to get the lowest available price.

If you are thinking of making your own offer to purchase a small number of shares, it does not matter very much whether you send it through a broker or an ECN. Either way, it will be accepted if it turns out to be the best offer on Nasdaq at some moment. If you pick a price somewhat above the best buy offer, you will have a good chance of being best, but also a good chance that your price will not be any better than if you just accepted the best sell offer. The problem is that the market is likely to move between the time you decide on your price and when it is posted. If the market moves up, your price will be down the list of buy offers and you will not make a deal. If the market moves down, your price will wind up close to the best sell offer.

Because you are likely to buy or sell at about the same price however you trade a small number of shares, the way to make the decision is on the commission you pay. Among brokers, you can pay hundreds of dollars to a "full-service" broker, $40 to Schwab, $20 to E*Trade, $8 to Ameritrade. Or you can pay $1 to Island, the cheapest ECN. The amount of hand-holding varies accordingly. ECNs have the most efficient technical operations and price their services to exploit it.

If you are buying thousands of shares, the situation is more critical. Outside investors may fall victim to abuse when they trade big positions. Common victims of naïve trading practices are founders of successful startups who cash out after IPOs.

Outside investors may fall victim to abuse when they trade big positions.

To understand the abuses, it is useful to start by looking at the practices of experienced traders working for large pension or mutual funds or for sophisticated seriously wealthy individuals. These traders sometimes run informal auctions over the phone to buy or sell large blocks of stock. They post offers in Instinet at carefully chosen prices and volumes, sometimes making use of a feature in Instinet that permits the customer to specify a hidden extra volume. And they trade with dealers with whom they have negotiated blanket discounts. They check the performance of dealers after the completion of trades to see that no abuses have occurred. For larger trades, Nasdaq is anything but an electronic system that automatically executes every customer's desired trade.

Consider the founder of a company that went public a few months ago, who wants to sell 100,000 shares for around $20 each. This is a big trade, especially since the total volume of trade in a new company is likely to be small. She could start accepting buy offers, most of which would be for a few hundred shares. As she worked her way through the buy offers available everywhere on Nasdaq, she would receive lower and lower prices. New offers to buy would come in to Nasdaq at lower prices, as people saw trades occurring at depressed prices. It would be wise for her to take her time, selling her shares over a period of weeks.

Suppose our founder told a broker to sell her 100,000 shares. The broker would probably say, "This is a big order. It will take us some time to work it. And the price won't be as good as the current price." That much is honest. The danger is what comes next. It is sadly common for the broker and affiliated dealer to start selling shares they own or have borrowed before they do anything for the customer. The broker and dealer work their way down the existing offers, selling at lower and lower prices. Then, at the end, they buy the customer's shares all at once at the low price. The broker and dealer, not the customer, benefit from the higher prices that the earlier sales command. Figure 5-2 illustrates how this abuse occurs.

When a broker/dealer sells from its own account after learning that a customer wants to sell, but before buying the shares from the customer, it is "trading ahead of the customer" or "front-running." The practice is contrary to the rules of Nasdaq and violates securities law, but is still thought to be common for large

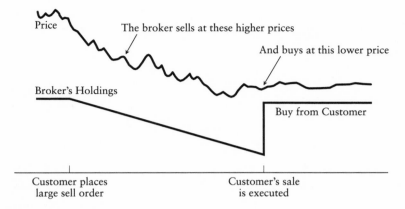

Figure 5-2. Front Running

A customer places a large sell order with a broker. The broker holds the order while selling shares. The sales push the price down. Then the broker buys the shares from the customer by executing the order. Though the order is executed at the market price at the time, the customer could have sold at better prices earlier. The broker pockets the difference.

trades. Enforcement of the rule against front-running is not effective, because the penalty to a broker/dealer who is caught is relatively slight—refunding the customer's loss. Customers are not allowed to sue brokers or dealers in court. They can only complain to the National Association of Securities Dealers, an organization that tends to side with its members rather than with customers. And there are many ways for dealers to front-run in ways that are difficult to detect.

Quite apart from the possibility of becoming the victim of front-running, it does not make sense for a customer to turn over to a broker the job of managing a large trade. The equivalent in the real estate market would be to tell a broker that you want her to sell your house and get a good price, without your remaining involved to consider the offers that come in. Your trading manager should be someone you trust completely and someone you monitor closely. That's the way large funds operate.

The temptation to front-run the customer will exist in any e-market where an agent like a broker sits between the customer and the market. Knowledge of a new large purchase or sale on an e-market is valuable to the agent. Only a closely supervised and monitored agent will decline the opportunity to gain from the knowledge, at the customer's expense.

Market Orders in Nasdaq

In most markets, there are customers who want to delegate thinking about the right price to others more knowledgeable than themselves. They are usually smaller players, buying or selling something that is not central to their businesses or lives. Rather than shopping carefully, these customers want to receive the market price, whatever it is. In the stock market, many individual investors take this view.

Nasdaq has rules that make it safe and reasonable to buy and sell without specifying a price, provided that your trade is a few hundred shares and not thousands. You can place an order with a broker to buy or sell a stated number of shares at the market price—a *market order*. Such an order is functionally the same as accepting the best pending offer. As I noted before, the chances are that the seller who posted the best pending offer will not be the source of the shares that you purchase with a market order. Rather, your market order will be filled by your broker's affiliated dealer, but at the best pending price, not the dealer's current offer. This rule appears to be successfully enforced.

The Role of Dealers in Nasdaq

> The principle of natural selection operates with a vengeance among dealers.

In general, a dealer is a business that buys low and sells high. Its income arises from its ability to spot low and high prices, and to buy when the price is low and sell when it is high. Dealers are specialists at discerning these opportunities. The principle of natural selection operates with a vengeance among dealers—if a dealer can't buy low and sell high, it will be out of business soon. The presence of dealers in a market confirms that the outside players leave some cash on the table—they have more important tasks than spotting the small opportunities that dealers live off.

Dealers differ from customers because dealers post offers in the same stocks all the time. Other customers post their offers only when they have some reason to trade; dealers are ready to trade all the time. Dealers hold inventories of the stocks for which they make markets. If some big sales deplete the inventory, a dealer will buy from other players—customers, other dealers, or ECNs—to restore a normal inventory level. Furthermore, dealers are also players in the market. If one dealer thinks another player is offering a favorable price, the dealer will buy or sell. If a dealer receives an informative tip about a stock, the dealer will buy if the tip is good news for the company or sell if bad news. Dealers are not just mechanical buyers and sellers.

Brokers are people or businesses who take orders from individual investors. Brokers are often dealers as well or, if not, they have contracts with dealers. The economic forces binding brokers to dealers are profound. They originate from the fundamental principle of e-commerce that players will conceal their best prices. Dealers' offers are displayed to the public. They are not the dealers' best prices. But there is no general opportunity for dickering in Nasdaq. The contracts between brokers and dealers—or the equivalent relationships achieved by combining the broker and dealer functions in one company—solve the problem of getting a better price than is shown in the quotes.

Suppose that Nasdaq did support dickering for each trade. As we will see, some investors would receive better prices than others, even if they were trading the same number of shares and had the same bargaining skills. Because the same situation may arise in many other types of e-commerce, it is important to understand how an e-market can adjust to these systematic differences among customers.

Discounts on Nasdaq

A dealer in a posted-offer exchange is like the car dealer mentioned in chapter 1 who doesn't dicker and sets the same price for everybody. The dealer will not post a price as good as the one that the best-informed and most skilled customer would be able to extract. The expert customers will take their business else-where unless there is some way to overcome this disadvantage.

The problem will be compounded if some customers are cheaper to serve than others (I'll discuss later in this chapter why this is the case in the stock market).

A powerful tool for attracting expert customers is the *blanket discount*. Rather than dicker over each transaction, why not dicker once and for all over a discount to be applied uniformly to all business with a customer? As I noted in chapter 1, this kind of discount appears all over the economy. It makes the posted-price market a viable competitor to the dickered market, whether traditional or automated. Blanket discounts are widespread in Nasdaq.

Who would get the best deals in Nasdaq if there were dickering? In the stock market, some players know a lot more than others. This knowledge is dangerous to dealers. Suppose a customer knows that a company has just signed a major customer, or just made a technical breakthrough, but the news has not yet reached the market. The customer can buy the company's stock by accepting the dealer's offer to sell. Later, the dealer has to replace that stock. If the news reaches the market in the meantime, the dealer will pay more for the replacement stock than the earlier sale price. The round-trip will cost the dealer money, whereas dealers normally make their living by selling stock for more than it costs to replace. A similar loss occurs when an informed investor sells just before bad news reaches the market. Informed investors are a fact of life in the stock market. Information makes its way from the confidential activities of businesses to employees, contractors, and friends.

Another major flow of information comes from large players such as mutual and pension funds. The news that a fund plans to buy a large position in a stock is valuable because the purchase will drive the price up. As a result, many of the informed traders are in the securities business and are not in direct contact with

> The blanket discount is a powerful tool for attracting expert customers.

the company about whose stock price they have secret information.

Dealers protect themselves against informed traders by setting higher offers to sell and lower offers to buy than they would in a market without the leakage of secrets. The loss from selling to these traders is smaller if the selling price is higher, and the loss from buying from one of them is smaller if the buying price is lower. Thus the spread—the difference between the buy offer and the sell offer—is widened by the presence of informed traders.

In Nasdaq, dealers' offers are not best prices; the principle of concealing your best price forbids it. The quotes are the dealers' worst prices, those charged to the traders most likely to be informed and positioned to victimize the dealers. The dealers are willing to trade with others at more favorable prices. If there were dickering in Nasdaq, customers who could show that they were probably not informed would be able to negotiate better prices. Those safe customers are institutions and retail brokerage customers. They are not plugged into company secrets, and they do not have information about impending trades except their own.

Nasdaq does give safe customers better prices. Institutions get better prices by dickering on the phone. Individual investors, who are generally safe customers, get theirs through blanket discounts. The discounts are negotiated between brokers who handle trades for retail customers and Nasdaq dealers. Although blanket discounts are an uncontroversial fact of life in traditional B-to-B commerce, the discounts in Nasdaq have been challenged for resembling illegal kickbacks. The discounts in Nasdaq are called *payment for order flow*. A dealer pays brokers a few pennies per share for agreeing to direct all of their retail customers' orders in specified stocks to the dealer. The reason for the controversy is that the broker receives the discount, not the customer. Market forces should cause the discount to flow to the retail customer in the form of lower commissions on trades, but some critics nonetheless challenge the practice of payment for order flow. What matters for e-commerce is just that blanket discounts, possibly taking the form of payment for order flow, will occur in any exchange where customers pay posted prices and do not dicker over each transaction.

Another important feature of trading in Nasdaq stocks is that large volumes of trades occur outside the Nasdaq system. The rules of the Securities and Exchange Commission require that all of these trades be disclosed almost as soon as they occur. That is, regulation requires a high degree of transparency in Nasdaq. As in other electronic markets, transparency is taken to be a goal of its own; it has not been demonstrated that the regulation requiring the publication of prices and quantities for all trades is actually desirable.

Electronic Exchanges in Nasdaq Stocks

Nasdaq evolved in the reverse of the order likely to be seen in new e-markets. Originally, the Nasdaq had only traders—customers and dealers. The only exchange was the primitive system for displaying the best offers of each dealer. Electronic exchanges such as Instinet and Archipelago came later and have diverted a substantial fraction of the dealers' business. Modern e-markets are likely to evolve in the opposite order. After an e-market based on an exchange comes into being, dealers will begin to operate on the e-market. In chapter 2, I described the huge dealer community that eBay has created.

Instinet and the other ECNs are pure exchanges; they do not hold any inventories of shares themselves. Their revenue comes from small commissions—such as Island's $1 per trade of any size—that traders pay. Although originally Instinet accepted only institutions as members—so that its members could be reasonably confident that they were trading with safe players—later it allowed dealers to become members and trade on the exchange. Dealers use Instinet in large volumes to balance their inventories. One of the important attractions of Instinet for dealers is that they can post offers anonymously. Their offers on Nasdaq itself cannot be anonymous.

Instinet announced a plan to permit individual investors to trade on their exchange, but retracted the plan at the beginning of 2001. The plan would have been beneficial to investors—I hope that it is revived soon.

The ECNs do not identify the customer who has posted an offer. They are anonymous exchanges. Institutional members used to be able to mark their offers as institutional only, so they were invisible to dealers. This gave an institution protection against dangerous dealers who have secret information. As in other e-markets, the questions of whether to provide information about participants and, if so, how much information are subtle ones that have to be worked out by experience. In completely anonymous electronic stock markets—for example, in Toronto—much trading of larger positions has moved out of the e-market and back to traditional dickering over the phone because players prefer to know who is on the other side. On the other hand, Nasdaq dealers love Instinet because they can buy anonymously.

> Nasdaq shows that dealers and exchanges can coexist efficiently.

What are the lessons of Instinet for e-markets? First, a neutral exchange may develop and flourish within a system originally designed as a dealer system. Nasdaq shows that dealers and exchanges can coexist efficiently. One will not drive the other out of business, though ECNs have taken a big chunk of business from the dealers. Second, groups of customers of an exchange may elect, for good reasons, to trade with each other only and to exclude others from seeing their postings on the exchange. Forced centralization of an exchange, with all postings available to all participants, may not be the best answer.

Nasdaq has not yet reached equilibrium—the ECNs are still growing at the expense of the dealers. It remains to be seen what fraction of customer business will come to ECNs rather than to dealers once equilibrium is reached.

Further Improvements in Nasdaq

Nasdaq does not provide a good solution today for the outsider buying or selling a large block of stock. Imagine an exchange where you could advertise that you are a private investor planning to buy 500,000 shares of Wal-Mart over the coming month, and inviting proposals from sellers. You could watch the offers come in and accept the ones with the best prices. Or suppose you could announce that you were planning a purchase auction 30 days from now. You will receive bids on a Saturday at 3:00 P.M. and announce the winners instantly. These kinds of tools would benefit individual investors who are buying or selling large blocks. Auctions would also benefit big funds, though they are already better served than individuals because of their ability to run informal auctions among large potential traders over the phone. The funds also get a good deal of protection from repeated trading with the same dealers; if a dealer front-runs an institution, the institution can take its business to another dealer next time.

Applications of the Nasdaq Model

Nasdaq is stripped down and streamlined for a good reason: stocks trade in fast-moving markets in huge numbers of mostly small transactions. Nothing like Nasdaq has evolved outside the stock market. A business plan to extend Nasdaq-style trading to semiconductors or freight scheduling or other arenas needs to take careful note of the limitations of the Nasdaq model.

Nasdaq is viable without supporting dickering over each trade. There are two reasons for its success in trading stocks despite its lack of any direct method for overcoming traders' reluctance to offer their best prices. First, the market for all but the most thinly traded stocks is pretty competitive. Players have to reveal something close to their best prices in order to attract trades at all, because there are many others willing to trade. Second, stock prices move so quickly that alternatives like auctions are not very popular. High price volatility drives investors toward immediate trading and away from periodic auctions. And informal auctions based on RFQs—widely used in less volatile B-to-B settings—would be cumbersome in Nasdaq because responses would be stale by the time they were received and assimilated.

Because dickering is the time-proven way to overcome the reluctance to disclose a best price up front, and because other markets don't move anywhere near as fast as the stock market, it seems unlikely that other markets will copy Nasdaq. Formal auctions, as at eBay or FreeMarkets, or informal ones based on offer/RFQ-bid-accept models are likely to dominate most e-markets.

Although the Nasdaq model is unlikely to spread far beyond the stock market, the close study of Nasdaq is essential to understanding e-markets in general. The web of relationships and contracts supporting blanket discounts is most fully developed in Nasdaq and is sure to exist in many other e-markets. Abuses based on trading by agents in advance of trading for their customers can exist in any market where agents have a role. The coexistence of dealers and customers is a feature of most e-markets as well.

A contest between e-markets and dealers is going on in Nasdaq. Pure e-markets, where investors trade directly with each other, are growing. The biggest and oldest is Instinet, but others, such as Island and Archipelago, are on the move. But the dealers will not disappear from Nasdaq. There will always be a role for a nimble mind guessing when stocks are cheap on the e-market and when they are expensive.

Half.com

Half.com is an arm of eBay. Unlike its parent, it sells products with a real-time deal engine. It is a Nasdaq ECN of used books, videos, and CDs. Sellers post offers for the objects they are selling. The service gets its name from the rule that you can't set a price offer above half of the list price of the object when it was new. As in Nasdaq, a purchaser has only one action—accepting the posted offer. No dickering can occur on Half.

Here is the offer book for Tom Petty's *Greatest Hits* CD on September 29, 2000:

Like new	Very good	Good	Acceptable
$7.58	6.99	7.49	6.90
7.59	7.50	8.97	
7.59	7.50		
8.92	7.51		
8.95	7.98		

As in Nasdaq, a customer can accept any order, but is most likely to accept the order with the best price. The people who offered the high prices of $8.92 and $8.95 for like-new copies are unlikely to make sales if there is a continuing flow of offers at the lower price around $7.59.

Half.com had 5.3 million listings the day I pulled off this table of offers. eBay paid $241 million in stock for Half in mid-2000. The site does a considerable flow of business, even though it does not support dickering. Why does it attract business even though an auction or other form of dickering would do a better job? Why are the buyers willing to settle for the offered price, when they know it is not the seller's best price? Recall that there are two reasons for streamlined deal engines: (1) buyers want immediacy—they don't want to wait for an auction to close or for some other dickering process to reach its end—and (2) the items for sale are standardized and not too expensive. Both reasons apply to books, videos, and CDs. When you have found a video you like, you would prefer to wrap up the deal on the spot and have it shipped, rather than waiting for an auction to end. The hassles of dickering are large in relation to the $8 or so that you pay for a used CD and even less for most books.

The organization of Half.com encourages competition among the people posting price offers. You know the prices you have to beat in order to be likely to make a sale. This competition is intense for the most popular CDs, where dozens of offers appear on the site. The competition forces sellers to set prices closer to their best prices and helps overcome the lack of dickering.

It's interesting to speculate about the future of Half.com's business model. Suppose there were a number of rivals operating similar sites. Then customers would be interested in a site that aggregated, say, the three best offers for each CD from each of the rival sites. They would want the equivalent of the Nasdaq montage for CDs. Customers could find the best deal from the aggregation site without having to visit all of the sites offering used CDs. But Half.com, presumably the biggest of the sites, would resist providing its offers to the aggregation site. Squabbles would erupt about who owns the information about the offers, just as they have in Nasdaq and in online auctions. Chapter 8, on intellectual-property rights, will take a further look at this issue.

T A K E A W A Y S

- **Real-time deal engines satisfy the demand for immediacy.** In a real-time engine, a customer can accept a displayed offer and make an immediate transaction. Customers in the fast-moving stock market desire immediacy.

- **Nasdaq, the leading e-market exchange, is a system for posting offers to trade.** An investor can check the best posted offer or post her own offer. Most of the transactions in Nasdaq are between dealers who have posted offers and outside investors who are accepting them.

- **Within Nasdaq, the electronic communications networks are deal engines that permit investors to review and accept existing offers or to post their own offers.** ECNs like Instinet make it possible for investors to trade with each other rather than using dealers as intermediaries. The ECNs have lower costs and charge less for trades.

- **Outsiders with larger trades face the danger of front-running.** A broker may delay filling a customer's large order and trade himself in order to profit from the price change that the order causes.

- **Dickering occurs in Nasdaq stocks, but not within the Nasdaq e-market.** Nasdaq does not support communication about price from one trader to another. Because the price offers posted on Nasdaq are not best prices, there is a payoff to dickering, but only for larger trades.

- **Half.com is a rapidly growing Nasdaq of CDs, videos, and books.** Half posts customer offers to sell, and other customers can accept offers and make immediate deals.

6

Posted
Prices

espite the excitement about online auctions and exchanges with deal engines that automate dickering, there is a huge role for the simplest e-market model, selling at posted prices. This model flourishes in markets where the seller specifies the product and has many customers for the same product. The buyer does not have other suppliers for the same product or does not buy enough of the product to make automated dickering through a procurement auction worth the trouble.

Big companies are moving huge amounts of B-to-B sales to e-markets. Eastman Chemical sells about $200 million per year of its products through Internet orders; IBM, about $20 billion. The e-market model for almost all of this commerce is the posted price. A customer buys millions of dollars worth of chemicals or computers in much the same way that you buy a book from Amazon. Established customers, especially those with high volumes, probably receive blanket discounts negotiated offline. Eastman does have auctions for unusual situations, but the quoted-price model dominates its online sales.

One common feature of posted-price e-markets is price discrimination. Different customers pay different prices for the same product. Another is product differentiation; sellers aim for different segments of the market. Some have high service and high prices; others have plain pipe racks and low prices. Online bookstores provide a good example of differentiated e-market sellers. Amazon is at the high end of price and service; 1BookStreet is at the low end of price.

e-Markets are fertile ground for real-time pricing strategies.

e-Markets are fertile ground for real-time pricing strategies, where the instant communication power of the Internet enables sellers to change their prices daily to track market changes, including changes in their rivals' prices. The airline e-market is a leading example.

All sellers face a tradeoff between volume and profit margin. A high-margin strategy generally yields a low volume, while a high-volume strategy comes at the cost of a low margin. In the music business, CDs are sold on a low-volume, high-margin business model. The e-market in digital MP3 downloads is forcing the music business to develop a low-margin, high-volume outlet.

Finally, e-market equilibrium often includes dealers. These players spot underpriced products, buy them, and then sell them when the time is ripe. eBay and Nasdaq are just two of the many e-markets with active communities of dealers.

Catalogs and Blanket Discounts

Not every e-market needs auctions, the Nasdaq model, the Priceline model, or the Half model. The simple structure of a catalog with posted prices works fine in many lines of e-commerce, with the addition of blanket discounts negotiated every year or so.

Many thriving e-businesses such as Grainger.com use the catalog-plus-blanket-discount model.

Negotiations over blanket discounts take place between executives of the customer and the dealer. Customers with higher volumes, better bargaining skills, and lower customer support costs will get the highest discounts. Then employees of the customer will order from the catalog, and the purchasing company will automatically receive the blanket discount. Office.com has adopted precisely this business model for office products.

Posted-quote exchanges will flourish in settings where there is only one supplier of a product or where the value of each purchase is relatively small, as in office products. Another factor favoring posted quotes without dickering is the prevalence of competition in the market. When there are many sellers of the same standardized product, their posted quotes will be close to their best prices because of strong competition. Again, this factor pushes the stock market and e-commerce in office supplies toward the posted-quote model and away from dickering each transaction.

Price Discrimination

Price discrimination occurs when different customers pay different prices for the same product. Price discrimination pervades all markets, and e-markets are no exception. It's a serious misunderstanding of e-markets to conclude—as some observers have—that the ease of price comparisons on the Internet suppresses price discrimination.

e-Markets are probably increasing the amount of price discrimination in the airline business, a topic taken up later in this chapter. Business travelers often pay two or even four times as much for a seat in the same cabin as pleasure travelers. Two new e-market pricing tools—the Internet special fare and the Priceline model—allow airlines to fill up otherwise empty seats with last-minute low-fare travelers without eroding their extraordinary profits from last-minute high-fare business travelers. Priceline is a good example of a pricing device that is immune to price comparisons—you can't find out the price without making a transaction.

Recall that in Nasdaq, market makers discriminate in favor of retail investors and mutual and pension funds—safe customers who are unlikely to cost market makers money by selling in advance of bad news or buying in advance of good. In e-markets such as Nasdaq or MRO products, where customers negotiate blanket discounts, the customers who are cheapest to serve will be able to negotiate the best discounts.

e-Market technology could bring price discrimination to a new height.

When a seller posts firm prices, as in the Amazon retail model, customers generally expect that all customers see the same price. In an early scene in *Casablanca,* a salesman in the souk shows Ingrid Bergman a lace tablecloth. He holds a price tag against it. When she shakes her head, he tries a different price tag. Customers in modern markets expect that the posted prices don't have this opportunistic character. You are confident that Costco displays the same price to everybody, and therefore infer that it must be a good price. On a web site, you can't be so sure. When customers discovered evidence that Amazon was using the souk pricing model rather than the Costco model, outrage followed.

In an e-market, the seller may be tempted to consult a database for information about a customer and set a special price accordingly. A customer who has shown signs in the past of shopping carefully for price gets a good price, while an impulse buyer gets a higher price. e-Market technology could bring price discrimination to a new height. But there are good reasons for a seller to avoid this kind of pricing. Shoppers understand the Costco pricing model. If they are not going to dicker for a purchase, they want to know what the deal is. Price discrimination should not be a secret. Senior discounts, student discounts, and frequent-purchase discounts are fine if they are not clandestine.

It is an important assurance that the customer is getting a good deal if a seller commits to its disclosed pricing policy. If a seller cuts special secret deals with some customers, it stands to reason that the deal the other customers get is not as good. So the rational shopper planning to buy at the posted price stays away from places with opaque pricing models.

Price discrimination is not illegal, nor is it economically harmful. A law compelling equal pricing to all customers would raise the prices charged to favored customers by as much as it would lower the price to the disfavored ones. There is no reason to expect a net benefit from a law against discrimination, even if it were practical to enforce it.

The Zero-Profit Principle

Profit is the driving force of all business, in e-markets as anywhere else. In equilibrium, there is no money left on the table—no opportunity for profit left unexploited. The unrealistic values awarded in the stock market to Internet pioneers in 1999 failed to recognize the force of this proposition. Competition in a market grows until the prospective profit is not high enough to cover the costs of starting yet another business in the market. I call this the *zero-profit principle.* It's key to understand that the seller with zero profit is the last one in—the pioneer may remain quite profitable. The principle does not condemn Amazon to zero profit but only a would-be rival entering Amazon's market today.

The zero-profit principle is one of the basic ideas of modern economics. The principle applies in any market where there is no legal limit on entry to the business. Markets differ in the number of sellers that are viable at the zero-profit equilibrium. In some markets, sellers don't compete aggressively on price, but rather offer differentiated products. In these markets, numerous sellers may inhabit the market in equilibrium. The car market is a good example—a dozen or so carmakers with hundreds of models are viable in the U.S. and world markets. Among e-markets, the online market for books has this character. In other markets, even a second seller may have trouble attracting enough business to make a profit. The pioneer has an advantage over any later arrival. The market for personal computer operating systems provides an example of this kind of monopoly—no product can make significant headway against Microsoft Windows. Among e-markets, consumer auctions seem to have this character. eBay, the pioneer, dominates auctions, and the runner-up, Yahoo, has secured only a quarter of the business even though it gives its product away for free.

Price Comparisons and Extreme Competition

For products sold at posted prices, it's a lot easier to compare prices on the Internet than in traditional markets. Not only can you visit the sites of the sellers of books, CDs, videos, and other posted-price products, but you can use a price-comparison service such as mySimon to check many sites at the same time. If shoppers cared only about price, they would flock to sites with the lowest prices.

In that setting, an irresistible hydraulic pressure would press prices downward. One seller could shave the price of a CD a few cents below other sellers and capture all the business. But then another seller would undercut by another few cents and the business would shift again. The process of price-cutting would end only when profit margins fell close to zero. Extreme competition with low prices seems the inevitable outcome of a market where it is easy to find the seller with the lowest price.

Pundits have declared that extreme competition will be the rule after the Internet revolution is complete. They foresee more and more intelligent shopping bots able to track down the best deal for every kind of product. The main reason the pundits are badly wrong is the one stressed throughout this book—sellers don't post their best prices for the great majority of commerce.

You have to dicker to get the best price. Moreover, your dickering has to be in good faith; it has to be more than a ruse to find out the best price. In an auction, for example, you make a binding bid before you find out what the price will be.

The other reason the forecast of extreme competition is off base is that customers don't gravitate exclusively to the seller with the lowest price. They care about other aspects of the transaction: How easy is it to use a web site? How likely is it that the seller will fail to fill your order because it is out of stock? How easy is a return? How many other purchases can be made at the same site and shipped together, to save shipping costs? The online book market well illustrates the second reason.

> Customers don't gravitate exclusively to the seller with the lowest price.

Books Online

Online bookselling illustrates market equilibrium with numerous differentiated sellers selling at posted prices, governed by the zero-profit principle. Booksellers do not compete intensively with each other. If they did, extreme competition would prevail: prices would be the same at all sellers, and prices would be low everywhere. Instead, customers are loyal to their favorite sellers. Most of them continue to use Amazon despite lower prices from reputable alternatives such as 1BookStreet. Amazon puts huge efforts into retaining loyalty by offering a slick site, recommendations, a wide product line, and the like.

Anybody can start another bookselling web site. Accordingly, web sites will keep appearing until there is no profit left for another new site. Specifically, the zero-profit principle teaches that the market is in equilibrium when all businesses currently in the market are making enough money to keep them in business, but a prospective new business in the same market would make a loss.

Books are cheap, uniform products sold at posted prices—

along with CDs, videos, and electronic games. Amazon pioneered e-markets in these products and continues to be the largest seller, despite numerous competitors. These include bn.com (Barnes and Noble), Borders.com, 1BookStreet, and dozens of others. In addition, customers use general-purpose shopping bots, such as mySimon, and book shopping bots, such as BookBlvd and BookFinder. It is not hard to find information about prices, shipping costs and shipping delays, and evaluations of performance by other shoppers.

If e-markets tend toward price uniformity as a general matter, the tendency should be strongest in books, a fully developed e-market. Figure 6-1 shows pricing data gathered on August 6, 2000, from a wide variety of online booksellers, for a selection of books:

Author	Title	Format	List price
Jane Austen	*Emma* (Penguin edition)	Paper	7.95
Patrick O'Brian	*Fortune of War*	Paper	13.95
Mario Puzo	*Omerta*	Hardback	25.95
Andy Rathbone	*Upgrading and Fixing PCs for Dummies*	Paper	19.99

The prices in the figure include standard three- to seven-day shipping by U.S. mail or UPS. It is important to include shipping costs because the custom has developed in online bookstores of quoting low price before shipping but adding a compulsory shipping charge well above the actual cost of shipping. The figure does not reflect the lower shipping costs you would enjoy if you bought more than one book at a time.

In addition to online prices, figure 6-1 shows the actual prices of the books in the Barnes and Noble store on Fifth Avenue in New York (I believe Barnes and Noble charges the same prices in all of its stores). One fact stands out immediately—books are cheaper in the store than online. Books are uniformly more

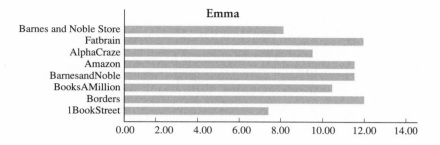

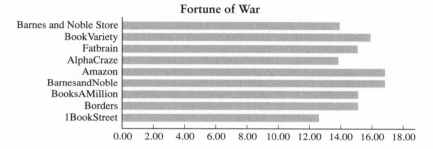

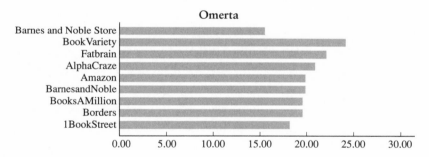

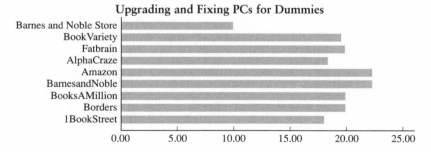

Figure 6-1. Book Prices

Books are almost always cheaper in the bookstore. Prices vary substantially across online sellers. The big online sellers, Amazon and Barnes and Noble, have intermediate prices, neither the highest nor the lowest.

expensive at bn.com than in the Barnes and Noble store, generally by a substantial margin. For example, *Emma* costs its list price of $7.95 in the store and $11.44 on the web. So intense competition on the Internet has not driven book prices to low levels. People will save quite a bit of money if they can buy books when they happen to be in a place that sells the books they want. The advantage of online sales is avoiding a special trip to the bookstore; for most people, it is better to pay Amazon $11.44 than drive to a bookstore, even if the store is nearby.

Figure 6-1 shows a remarkable amount of diversity in prices among online sellers. All of the sellers in the figure have the highest three-star rating for performance from Gomez, a rater of Internet vendors. Yet you can save a significant amount of money by buying the books from 1BookStreet rather than from Amazon, and you can save money on all but *Omerta* at AlphaCraze. People who buy books by price, and search with a shopping bot, will rarely buy from Amazon. Yet Amazon is by far the largest online bookseller. There is no suggestion in the data that the ready availability of shopping bots and the ease of determining prices on the Internet result in convergence of prices at a low level across sellers.

The only convergence in prices is the remarkable fact that the prices charged by Amazon and bn are identical to the penny for all four books. The two largest sellers have converged, but at relatively high prices. Is it suspicious that the two have identical prices? Is there some kind of implicit deal between Amazon and bn to set identical prices and avoid destructive competition? There is no way to tell from the data. Both collusion and the most vigorous competition result in identical prices.

The online sellers in figure 6-1 fall roughly into three categories. The three most powerfully branded sellers, Amazon, bn, and Borders, have intermediate levels of prices. They are high-service web sites, with many features that help glue their customers to them and avoid defections to sites with lower prices. Then 1BookStreet, BooksAMillion, and AlphaCraze compete on price, with less-well-known brand names. Finally, FatBrain and

BookVariety are specialty sites, with higher prices than the majors. Although no volume data are available, it is my impression that the specialty sites have relatively low levels of sales. They are not terribly profitable despite their high prices.

In a market like online bookselling where more than one business model is viable, the zero-profit principle applies separately to each model. There will be zero profit to a prospective Amazon clone, zero profit to a prospective low-price, low-service site, and zero profit to a high-price niche site.

The zero-profit principle does *not* say that all of the existing businesses in the market make no profit. In some markets, early entrants establish powerful brands that make them profitable beyond the level needed to keep them in the market—for example, Coca-Cola makes enviable profits even though it is almost certainly true that a business trying to launch a new major cola brand would not make money. One of the interesting mysteries of the online book business is whether Amazon's book business is profitable. Its operating results are buried in Amazon's total financials for all its lines, and include a large amount of business-development expense that obscures the profitability of its established book business.

The zero-profit principle helps explain the landscape of the online book business. Niche sites are viable because they can charge high prices. They can cover their fixed costs with relatively low volumes. They are protected from further competition because an additional niche site would have to lower its prices to attract adequate business, but then would not cover its fixed costs. High-service, moderate-price sites like Amazon are protected from further competition by the costs of creating a brand and attracting customers who are loyal to the existing sellers in that space. And low-price, low-service sites are protected from further competition by their low profits per unit, a situation that requires a large scale to cover fixed costs.

The online book business faces a basic limitation in selling a physical product that requires delivery. People will continue to buy a substantial fraction of their books off shelves and racks because they are much cheaper that way. The book business is bracing for the influence of digital books, delivered immediately over the Internet. Will the book business be transformed as quickly by the e-book as the music business has been by the MP3? It's too soon to tell.

Dynamic Pricing

In traditional markets, pricing tends to be simple and static. In the days when grocery stores put price tags on products, prices changed only as often as inventory turned over, and everybody paid the same price unless he cashed in paper coupons. As electronic pricing has taken over, prices change more frequently, and price discrimination has become more aggressive and refined.

e-Markets generally have unlimited scope and technology for dynamic pricing. A web site can calculate a new individualized price for a customer every few seconds. I noted in the discussion of price discrimination that sellers need to be careful about individualized prices in order to preserve the credibility of posted prices. But there is still plenty of opportunity for customizing prices over time and among buyers, as the airline e-market demonstrates.

Air travel is an established e-market. Airlines have used computer reservations systems since the 1960s to issue tickets and keep track of reservations and seat assignments. The product traded in the air travel e-market is digital—the right to take a particular seat on a particular flight. An Internet e-market in airline tickets does not face the disadvantage of physical delivery that holds back e-markets for tangible goods.

The computer reservations systems currently used in the airline business are among the most sophisticated of posted-price exchanges. In United's computer system, there are a dozen different prices for the same flight from Los Angeles to New York, and those prices change every day or every week. The price changes are computed by software that monitors bookings, rivals' prices, and other information. Each holiday calls for a set of adjustments too.

One departure from the posted-price principle is the use of blanket corporate discounts, which are not adjusted in real time. The other is Priceline, which is an important and growing tool for overcoming the limitations of posted prices. Delta Airlines was a founding investor in Priceline; many other airlines now sell there. A group of airlines has started a rival to Priceline called Hotwire.

Priceline marks just a beginning toward a flexible e-market. One could imagine an ultimate e-market for space on planes. Here's one idea that has turned over in my head since I learned about eBay. InternetAir, a new airline, could create an exchange of the kind discussed in chapter 5 for all of its seats, opening six months before each flight. Each seat on each flight would have its own little market. InternetAir would post an offer for each seat at the beginning. Customers or dealers could accept the offer or make a counteroffer and gain control of the seat (notice that the counteroffer would be similar to offers that customers make today on Priceline). Later, any seat holder could offer it on the exchange. Customers who changed their plans might do this, or dealers who were holding seats. Shortly before flight time, there would be a final auction to be sure the seat was sold.

> Priceline marks just a beginning toward a flexible e-market.

This e-market would eliminate the two big inefficiencies of air travel: sold-out flights and empty seats. When a flight sells out, it means that people who place the highest value on its seats are unable to fly on it—there isn't any good way for them to persuade others with more flexible schedules to sell back their seats. When there are empty seats, there are almost always people who would benefit from flying and be willing to pay some price, though not the airlines' standard fare. The exchange would give the high-value traveler a way to bid her way onto the airplane. And it would give the airline a way to market otherwise empty seats by accepting low bids for them.

Experience with other exchanges like Nasdaq tells us some of the things that would happen if InternetAir set up an exchange. First, dealers would be active. Travel agents would function as dealers, buying seats they expected to sell at a profit to their customers (commissions for agents would be replaced by spreads between buying and selling prices, just as in Nasdaq). Other dealers would be speculators—those with a good sense of what seats were going to be more expensive than the market thinks. Inside information would be an issue, as in Nasdaq; somebody knowing a little early about the scheduling of a large convention in Las Vegas could buy in advance of the information and profit from it. Dealers would pay for order flow from travel agents who directed orders from customers who did not have this kind of inside information.

It's unlikely that InternetAir will launch with this business model. The exchange would deprive the airline of the most important source of profit in the business—charging business travelers higher fares than ordinary folks. All airlines follow this practice to some degree. If you book on United on Monday to fly from San Francisco to New York on Tuesday and return on Wednesday, you will pay about $2,100, against about $500 for the same round-trip booked 30 days in advance and staying over Saturday. Even Southwest, champion of low fares, gives you a better deal if you don't book at the last minute. Booking ahead by several weeks and staying over Saturday are the hallmarks of the low-value tourist—few business travelers are able to meet either restriction. So airlines are able to set low fares for people who would not travel at higher fares and, at the same time on the same flights, set high fares for people who place high value on their travel.

High business fares are eroded quite a bit by competition. Governments and large corporations negotiate blanket discounts that take away part, but not all, of the extreme business fares.

You can work around the highest business fares, for example, by taking one-stop flights instead of the nonstops you would prefer. You can take Southwest and other low-fare airlines on many routes. But airlines still make much more profit on business travelers. Part of the story is the same as for Amazon—people choose the higher-service, strongly branded seller like American over the cheap airlines. In addition, airlines have perfected loyalty programs based on mileage that deter flyers from shopping for bargains on each business trip.

So InternetAir would be better off by preventing business travelers from buying cheap seats at the last minute, at the same time that it would like to encourage low-value customers from doing that. As a result, InternetAir's business model is likely to resemble existing airlines', rather than bringing a full open exchange to its seat market.

Figure 6-2 shows how airlines set fares dynamically to segment the market between business and other travel and to adjust to changes in demand. The figure shows the fares for five round-trips, all leaving September 12. It shows two fares for each trip, one for a return on the next day and the other for a return a week later. The next-day return is the type of fare a business traveler would use and the next-week return is the type a pleasure traveler would use.

The horizontal axis of the figure is the number of days before the flight when the fare was quoted. All the fares were obtained from Travelocity.com, a leading Internet travel agent not affiliated with any airline.

Figure 6-2 shows the two main ways that airlines try to charge higher fares to business travelers; fares are generally higher if you don't stay over Saturday and if you book the fare close to departure. The price disadvantage for the business traveler is greatest for the transcontinental trip on United. Even if you book ahead by a month, you have to pay an amazing $2,157—almost $.50 per mile—for that trip. The fare goes up a bit if you book only one day ahead, as many business travelers do.

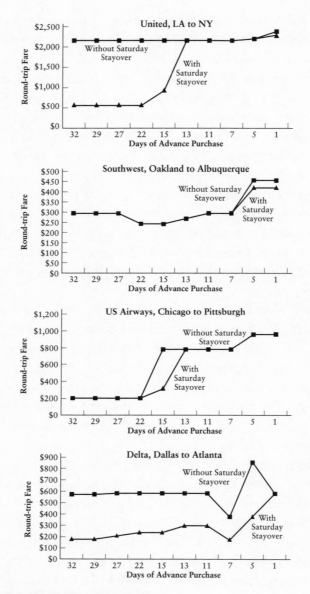

Figure 6-2. Fares for flights on September 12

All of the flights left on September 12 and returned either on the next day or a week later. The fares were quoted on Travelocity during late August and early September. The horizontal axis shows the number of days before the flight. Generally, you pay a higher fare if you buy close to the day of the flight. It's also generally cheaper if you stay over Saturday. These policies are ways of charging more for business travel.

The second panel of figure 6-2 shows Southwest's fares from Oakland to Albuquerque and return, a distance of just under 1,800 miles. Until a few days before departure, Southwest sets the same fare if you return the next day or stay over Saturday. Notice that the fare dropped substantially around day 22 and then rose again. Southwest was responding to changes in expected demand for seats on the flight, possibly as the result of a change in the fare of a rival on the route. An e-market permits immediate adjustments of prices whenever new information arrives. The goal of the adjustments is to fill every seat in the plane but not to leave any unsatisfied demand.

Southwest introduces a small amount of discrimination against business travelers in the last week before the flight leaves. Southwest's business model is at the opposite extreme from United's.

The third panel shows a US Airways flight from Chicago to Pittsburgh and return, a distance of 800 miles. The airline discriminates aggressively against business travel, using the book-ahead requirement rather than the Saturday stayover to keep the business traveler from using the leisure fare. The last-minute traveler pays an astonishing $1.20 a mile for the round-trip.

The bottom panel shows the 1,400-mile round-trip from Dallas to Atlanta on Delta. The upper line, showing the business fare without a Saturday stayover, goes through interesting gyrations in the last week. Seven days before departure, the computer foresaw empty seats and cut the fare. But two days later, that appeared to be a mistake, and the fare went up. Finally, on the day before the flight, the fare was back to the same level as for an advance booking. Unlike other airlines, Delta ramps the Saturday stayover fare upward day by day during the week before departure. The leisure traveler gets a break for staying over Saturday for all booking dates but the day before departure.

The data in figure 6-2 give some idea of the complexity and sophistication of pricing in the airline e-market. Airlines use advanced software to keep space available on flights to accommodate high-fare passengers who book at the last minute. Little of this would be possible outside of an e-market. If airlines published their fares in physical books distributed monthly to travel agents, they could not come close to the fine-tuning evident in the figure.

The airfare data illustrate a key point about e-markets: when prices are posted on a take-it-or-leave-it basis, without dickering, they can be completely flexible.

Posted prices can be completely flexible.

Despite the efforts to balance supply and demand through adjustment of fares, airlines still suffer from two major sources of lost profit: (1) flying empty seats and (2) turning away last-minute passengers willing to pay high fares for seats already filled with low-fare passengers. The airlines are turning to the Internet to solve these twin problems.

Many airlines now offer Internet specials to fill what would otherwise be empty seats. You can go to an airline's own web site and find fares that are not offered to travel agents—generally for travel within the next few days. Many of the fares are for round-trips over the coming Saturday, to fence them off from business travelers. These Internet fares are not so different from the idea of running an auction in an open exchange in order to fill up every flight. They are seriously limited, though, by the desire not to let business travelers in on the deal.

Why isn't there a market in airline tickets on eBay? This would be another neat solution to the problems of air travel. If you need to get to Pittsburgh the day after tomorrow, why not buy a ticket from somebody who got sick and can't go? Thousands of other kinds of tickets trade hands every day on eBay (including doctor.bob's Red Sox tickets). The answer is simple and absolute: there is a federal law against transferring airline tickets. The airlines have powerful lobbyists who would be sure to block any relaxation of the law. They would lose their ability to stick business travelers with higher fares if dealers could buy cheap tickets in advance and then resell them at the last minute to business types. The face of the airline industry would change completely in that case, even without an e-market.

The zero-profit principle applies to the airline industry, since there are few limitations on the entry of new airlines. The principle has the general implication that the benefits of improved efficiency pass ultimately on to the flying public, not to the airlines. Advancing e-markets that fill a larger share of the available seats make airlines more efficient. Even if the airlines don't pass the benefits on to the public right away, they change the calculus of the startup airline. Higher efficiency means higher profit and more startups, until additional competition pushes fares down.

The zero-profit principle tells something important about the likely effect of changes that reduced the differential between business and pleasure fares. Recall that there has to be enough profit in prices to keep the existing businesses in the market—if a price falls, it may result in a seller's departing the market for lack of adequate profit. A decline in business fares toward cheap fares would certainly have that effect. In the new equilibrium, with less competition, economy fares would have to be higher. It would not be a plain step forward to allow the reselling of tickets, for example. The large decrease in business fares that resulted would be offset by a smaller increase in economy fares (only about 7 percent of passengers actually pay the high business fares).

The Priceline Deal Engine

Priceline is another important tool for selling airline space at discriminatory prices. Priceline sells air travel, hotel space, and car rentals. The customer describes the product desired—travel destination and days—together with a proposed price. Priceline either accepts or declines the proposed price. The system does not support any further dickering. Priceline uses a posted-price e-market model, but with an important twist—the customer posts the price, and the seller decides whether or not to accept it.

Priceline accepts an offer if the proposed price is above a predetermined cutoff level. That minimum price is secret. Priceline adheres closely to the basic principle of concealing the best price that it will accept. And it sets rules that keep the price secret. For example, you can't start with a low price and work your way up until Priceline accepts your bid. Priceline prohibits a customer from bidding again on a particular product for a week. Although in principle customers who have had bids accepted on Priceline could share that information through a web site, there is actually almost no sharing. Priceline has truly succeeded in concealing its best prices.

The Priceline model does not impose a Saturday stayover (though that may be a factor in what bids an airline accepts—we don't have any way of knowing). Instead, it adds just the kind of friction that will drive away most business travelers. You have to wait for up to an hour to find out what booking you get on Priceline. You have little control over departure and arrival times. You may spend several hours at an airport along the way. Priceline is not a reliable way to get to your noon meeting in Minneapolis. But Priceline can fill up seats a few days before flight time.

Priceline has a unique e-market pricing model where customers post prices.

e-Commerce with posted quotes is a simple transplantation from store-based retail to an electronic equivalent. Staples.com looks a lot like a Staples store. But Priceline is a complete innovation—an application of the idea of posted offers in a totally novel way. Its success has caused a lot of new thinking about e-commerce business models, and it holds important lessons for fundamental issues in e-markets relating to the importance of opaqueness in some markets. The failure of Priceline's business model in other products—gasoline and groceries—is equally informative.

Priceline has been a huge success in terms of business volume, sufficient to draw Microsoft and a coalition of airlines into similar businesses. In late 2000, about 6 percent of all U.S. airline seats were sold through Priceline. As competition has broken out in Priceline's market, the company's future profit has fallen and its market capitalization has dropped to a more realistic value. In addition, Priceline unwisely tried to extend its model into markets such as groceries and gasoline where it did not belong, imposing huge losses on its shareholders.

The essence of Priceline's model is the secrecy of its best prices and of the prices paid by its customers. Priceline's choices of products are not accidental. Rather, air travel and hotels have an important market feature in common—under traditional sales methods, rivals know prices faster and better than do customers. Suppose Delta (a co-owner of Priceline) wants to attract more passengers to its New York to Atlanta flights. As soon as it makes a better fare available on reservations systems and advertises the fare, Continental (Delta's main rival on that route) will cut its fare to the same level. Delta will not be able to divert traffic from Continental. Instead, both airlines will lose profit.

Suppose that Delta leaves its posted fares unchanged but lowers its best price on Priceline. This move is a sneak attack on Continental. Delta will obtain a higher flow of travelers from Priceline without letting its rivals know why they are losing business.

Priceline's opacity—its model that conceals prices actually paid—is a huge step forward in improving competition in markets where other sales models result in public knowledge of prices. Commentary on Priceline has given its novel business model relatively little credit. Many reporters grumble that almost all Priceline customers pay more than Priceline's best price and thus more than Priceline pays to its suppliers. And press coverage has focused on the inevitable problems than result from the model's requirement that the customer commit to buying an incompletely specified product, especially in air travel. Because a major purpose of Priceline is to fill the empty seats on less popular flights, customers have to be prepared to leave early, arrive late, or make long layovers. But the benefits of filling seats that would otherwise be empty because of the limitations of existing methods for selling air travel are substantial, especially for short-notice travel where the airlines' desire to set extreme prices for

business travelers generally makes them forgo profitable opportunities to carry other passengers at lower fares. The following
posting from a web site devoted to consumer reactions to Priceline (positive and negative) tells the story nicely:

> I had to go home from Arizona to Bham [Birmingham] to see
> my grandmother before she died. This was a last minute travel
> arrangement. I was quoted anywhere from $750 to $1600 for
> a ticket since the 14 day advance purchase did not apply. The
> airlines could have cared less about my problem or concern to
> see my grandmother. I got my ticket thru priceline at $239.00
> roundtrip. I bid $198 for the ticket . . . so yes maybe they did
> add a few dollars to the price and yes I did have to go to Char-
> lotte and lay over an hour and a half to get to Bham . . . but I
> got to Bham in time to see my grandmother and I did not feel
> raped. I could not have made the trip had it not been for price-
> line. Thank you priceline. . . . The other thing the plane was
> only ⅔ full or less on all my flights so why couldn't the airlines
> have done the same directly. . . . I would have gone standby
> under the circumstances.

Priceline seems to work particularly well for hotels, where the
product is easier to specify than for air travel. Experienced users
of Priceline—who have figured out approximately what Priceline's cutoff prices are—report large savings off hotels' best
quoted rates.

Priceline teaches us that transparency is not necessarily a good
thing in e-markets or in any markets. It is the unavoidable transparency of traditional methods for selling air travel, hotels, and
similar products that results in empty seats and vacant rooms.
When prices are publicized, airlines and hotels can't fill their
seats and rooms without spoiling their existing business. They
would prefer to have 30 percent vacancies on the average. Priceline's opaqueness provides a way to overcome this obstacle to
full utilization.

Should large corporations use Priceline? Probably not. They

have another tool to achieve the same objective, the secret blanket discount. Every large corporation negotiates with airlines and hotels to pay prices that are based on the published prices but are discounted, often sharply.

Neutral Proposed Price

The National Transportation Exchange uses an e-market model suited to its business of matching freight carriers to shippers. When a shipper seeks transport for a truckload of goods, the exchange consults a database of information about its enrolled shippers and about actual shipping rates. The exchange matches the shipment to one of its shippers and proposes a price to both sides. If they both accept, the deal is made. As yet, the exchange is not a significant player in the freight business. Its novel e-business model seems like a good idea; it has inhabited economics textbooks for decades. But the model is not used elsewhere, to my knowledge.

Tickets for Games and Concerts

Like airline tickets, tickets for concerts and sports events are purely digital products, ripe for sale in e-markets. And these e-markets are growing rapidly. Every top-level professional sports team has a web site to sell tickets. So far, with only two exceptions I know of, these sites stick to traditional, simple, fixed posted prices. The stadium is divided into a few sections, and each section has the same price for any regular-season game. The result is lots of empty seats when the home team is out of favor and the visitor is boring, and a shortage of seats when hot teams play each other. Some teams—the Cleveland Indians—sell out every game while others—the Oakland As—

> Tickets are purely digital products, ripe for sale in e-markets.

leave seats empty for every game. During the 2000 season, the Seattle Mariners stimulated sales for three of their less popular games by online ticket auctions. In their auction, the best seats sold for well above the standard box office price. The San Francisco Giants run auctions for season tickets on sale by their original purchasers—again, desirable seats sell for far more than the standard price.

Teams leave a huge amount of money on the table by underpricing popular games. Economists have puzzled over this strange habit, as well as over the similar habit of restaurants of allowing demand to exceed supply chronically. Few big businesses have the same habit. I don't have a good explanation for underpricing. Like many fans, I frequently pay above box office prices for good games, especially playoff games, where the underpricing is laughable.

The Internet has a growing role in dealing with popular games where the demand for tickets at box office prices is greater than the supply. The e-market for sports tickets (and other events) is growing as fast as any e-market. There is a key difference between air travel, where the law forbids a secondary market, and the sports ticket market, where secondary e-markets flourish. A *secondary market* is one where the original seller—the baseball team—does not participate. The supply to a secondary market comes from people—dealers and others—who buy from the original seller and sell to the public.

The first hour that the Yankees start selling tickets for a new season, in December of the year before, dealers place orders with the box office for good tickets for all the Yankees-Mets games of the season. Fans who want those tickets and don't place their orders in December have to go to the dealers. New York law forbids reselling tickets for above face value, but it has almost no effect. Many dealers operate in Connecticut, where the law smiles on these transactions.

Traditionally, dealers at various scales have operated the secondary market, including the guys who stand around the stadium ready to transact. The dealers dicker with their customers.

But eBay is a huge new force in the secondary market. Dealers are active on both sides of eBay ticket auctions, as you can see by glancing over the experience ratings of the sellers and buyers in those auctions. The dealers don't respect the official rules of eBay the way ladylike sellers of Victorian collectibles do. Many dealers convert eBay into a posted-price market by telling bidders that the first bid automatically wins on the spot. The bid has to meet the stated minimum. So this dealer is acting just like a Nasdaq dealer posting a quote. It is also common for dealers to invite bidders to agree to pay more than the current visible auction price if the dealer closes the auction, which has the effect of reducing the fee the dealer pays eBay (a complete abuse).

eBay has a nominal rule against bids in New York and Massachusetts for above face value. Dealers get around the rule by auctioning a worthless baseball card along with valuable tickets. Ticket dealers treat eBay as a tool to be used in whatever way they can dream up. Designers of other e-markets need to keep in mind this tendency to find unexpected ways to use their market mechanisms.

eBay dominates ticket auctions in the same way that it dominates most other auctions. Attempts to create specialized sports ticket auctions, or to generate ticket auction business at other auction sites, have been unsuccessful.

The Volume-Margin Tradeoff

Purely digital products are the natural ones for Internet distribution. The sudden transformation of the music market in 1999, as the MP3 download became a standard way to obtain and trade music, is the leading example. A similar transformation will occur as digital movies become available on the Internet and users gain enough bandwidth to download them.

The headlines about MP3s relate to ownership. Is it legitimate for Napster to help fans copy songs from others without paying the owners of the songs? What about the 120,000 web sites that offer downloads of MP3s without regard to the copyrights of the owners? These intellectual-property questions are the subject of chapter 8. The conclusion is that the infrastructure already exists for marking music with copyright notices and enforcing ownership rights. As the infrastructure is deployed, the players in e-markets for music will need to negotiate the right to sell or give away the music files they offer. File-sharing technologies like Napster will check that a user has the right to copy music from another user.

As property rights in music become effective again and bandwidth becomes available to more and more fans, an e-market for digital music will emerge. Customers will pay for music. These e-markets will use the posted-price model—a digital song is a perfect example of a product sold by a single seller to many customers. The market will choose among many alternative applications of the principle of the posted price. Music will be sold as downloads to be stored on users' hard disks or MP3 players and played many times. Or it will be sold as digital streams, to be heard once but not captured. Prices for downloads will be much higher than for streams; a large volume of streamed music is already available on the Internet for free. In both cases, fans will choose between monthly subscriptions giving access to unlimited downloading or listening from a large catalog, or song-by-song selection at posted prices for each track.

The economic principle most important for understanding the emerging digital music market is the *volume-margin tradeoff*. Some businesses set high prices with high corresponding profit margins and accept low volumes. They are profitable because the high price generates a substantial margin on each sale, even though there aren't many sales. Other businesses set low prices and aim for high volume. The key point is that the two business models frequently coexist. We saw that already in the data on book prices, where some very low-volume sellers are viable because they can sell at high prices. In retailing, Costco uses the low-margin, high-volume model, competing with convenience stores that use the high-margin model. The phone company sells voice mail for $6 per month and does little business; Sprint PCS throws voice mail in for free. Apple sells computers for high margins and accepts a low market share; Dell accepts low margins and gets high volumes.

Figure 6-3 shows the volume-margin tradeoff in a graph. Price is on the horizontal axis. Margin is a straight line, rising with price. Volume is a downward-sloping curve, as customers buy lower volumes at higher prices. Profit is the product of margin and volume. Profit rises and then falls, reaching a maximum in the middle, but the profit curve is close to flat. The figure illustrates a high-margin, low-volume business model on the right and a low-margin, high-volume model on the left. They both make about the same amount of profit. There is no strong economic force pushing toward one model or the other.

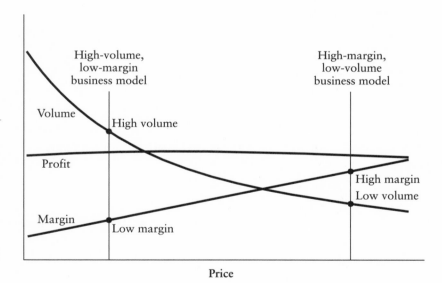

Figure 6-3. The Tradeoff between Volume and Margin

The upward-sloping line shows the margin, which rises with price. The downward-sloping line is volume, which falls as price rises. Profit is the margin times price, and first rises and then falls. The high-margin, low-volume business model is on the right, and the low-margin, high-volume business model is on the left. Profit is about the same for the two models.

One reasonably reliable generalization is that old, established sellers gravitate toward the high-margin, low-volume model while their new rivals counterattack with the low-margin, high-volume alternative.

The music industry combines the two models as well. CDs are the high-margin, low-volume channel for distributing music. Fans put out $16 for the CD only when they really want the album. Radio and TV—and now the Internet—provide the low-margin, high-volume channel. Music lovers sample new music from radio or MTV at zero cost and then buy the music they really like.

The MP3 is altering the traditional equilibrium of expensive and free music. In the old days, fans could make cassette copies of music from CDs or off the air, but now they can download MP3s, store them on disk, and make copies for friends. And with Napster, Gnutella, and similar peer-to-peer Internet facilities, you can let anyone in the world copy the MP3s from your computer. A huge expansion in the low-margin, high-volume part of the market is occurring.

So far, most of the effort of the record labels has been to defend the high margins of the CD business against the MP3 onslaught. Some of these companies have offered single tracks as digital downloads at prices around $2, about equivalent to CD pricing. Like most established sellers, they are afraid to sell at drastically lower margins because they do not anticipate large enough increases in volume to compensate.

A low-margin, high-volume model under discussion would give fans unlimited access to a large library of MP3s for a monthly charge of around $5. Although the evidence suggests that expanded MP3 usage has not diminished the demand for CDs, the record labels have not yet shown much interest in the new model.

The history of videotape provides a guide to the likely evolution of the digital music business. When the VCR first hit the market, moviemakers tried to outlaw it, just as the record labels have attacked Napster in court. Moviemakers feared that cheap home copies of movies would erode their high-margin theater business. In fact, the VCR became the basis of a hugely profitable extension of the movie business. The public much preferred factory recordings of movies over homemade. At first, videos were a high-margin product aimed at the rental market. Finally, it dawned on moviemakers that they could make even more profit from low-margin, high-volume sales of videos to consumers.

TAKEAWAYS

- **e-Markets with posted prices and blanket discounts account for huge and growing volumes of e-commerce.** Sellers of newly produced goods don't generally benefit from auctioning them, because conditions don't change much over time. They simply set prices. But they negotiate secret blanket discounts off those prices for each customer, except the small one.

- **Price discrimination—selling the same product to different customers at different prices—is an important feature of many posted-price business models.** For example, airlines sell the same seats at high fares to business travelers and at low fares to pleasure travelers.

- **Despite the availability of price comparison services, products such as books sold at posted prices show large variations in price across sellers.** Customers don't bother to shop intensively for a $15 item, or they value the services of the higher-priced sellers such as Amazon.

- **Dynamic posted prices are a key feature of the airline business model.** Fares for immediate travel are much higher than those for travel in a month or later. If a flight threatens to have empty seats, the airline can lower the fare, sometimes only for customers using the Internet.

- **The Priceline deal engine adds value in certain markets, such as air travel, hotels, and rental cars.** Because the Priceline user sets the price, the model avoids any disclosure of available prices. The Priceline model extends price discrimination in a valuable way, making it possible to offer low fares to some last-minute customers without cutting business fares.

- **Secondary markets using auctions or other deal engines will move in when posted-price e-commerce sets the wrong prices.** Tickets for sports and music events are a leading example—eBay does a large amount of business in tickets when the box office price is much too low.

- **The choice of business model needs to consider the volume-margin tradeoff carefully.** In recorded music, for example, the industry has traditionally sold CDs at high margins and low volumes. As music distribution moves into e-markets as digital downloads, the high-volume, low-margin alternative will probably generate higher value.

7

Antitrust and Regulation

Government provides key infrastructure for e-markets. Many of the roles of government are so deeply embedded in the economy that we hardly think about them. Government enforces private contracts—if it didn't, no form of business would function efficiently. e-Markets will thrive only in countries with effective governments. To see why, visit a country like Cambodia where the government hardly exists.

Law enforcement is one of the central functions of government. e-Markets could not function without laws against embezzlement and other business crimes. This chapter looks at one of the most controversial parts of law enforcement, antitrust. e-Markets have already been a hotbed of antitrust scrutiny and action, and new ones are sure to attract as much attention. Along with antitrust, the chapter will discuss regulation. In the two leading e-markets—airline tickets and the stock market—antitrust and regulation have worked in parallel to try to cure abuses that limited competition and raised prices.

Antitrust

Antitrust laws protect customers from high prices when business practices harm markets. The most blatant abuse is a conspiracy among suppliers to set prices at an agreed level, higher than would result from competition among the suppliers. The law focuses on particular abusive acts; it is not a violation of antitrust law to be a monopolist able to charge high prices, but it is a violation to achieve monopoly by harming competitors, making agreements with them, or taking them over.

The misconduct that antitrust law forbids falls into three main categories:

1. Agreements among competitors or between sellers and customers that reduce competition and raise prices (Sherman Act, section 1)
2. Acts of single firms that harm rivals in ways that will ultimately raise prices by creating a monopoly (Sherman Act, section 2)
3. Mergers or acquisitions that raise prices (Clayton Act, section 7)

Although I have stated that the objective in all three categories is to prevent high prices, an equal objective of antitrust law is to promote innovation. Misconduct that leaves prices unchanged but prevents customers from getting better products also runs afoul of antitrust law.

The law is just as concerned with misconduct among purchasers as among sellers. Agreements among purchasers that reduce the prices received by suppliers are illegal, in particular.

Antitrust enforcement has two forms. First, government agencies monitor the economy and take action against abuses that they find or that are reported to them. The Antitrust Division of the Department of Justice (DOJ) is the most prominent government antitrust watchdog, especially since its high-profile case against Microsoft. The Federal Trade Commission has a similar function. And each state has an attorney general who may take legal action under state antitrust laws, which typically track the federal laws.

The second form of antitrust enforcement is the private antitrust case. Many private cases follow in the tracks of earlier government cases. For example, the software maker Caldera—holder of rights to the old rival to Microsoft DOS called DR DOS—sued Microsoft and received a settlement of several hundred million dollars. Caldera's case followed closely a case that the DOJ had developed against Microsoft earlier. In 1994, Microsoft agreed with the DOJ to discontinue practices that had been harmful to DR DOS and other operating systems in the late 1980s.

Antitrust laws are one of the fundamental features of the economy that condition business decisions. Anytime a business makes an agreement with its rivals, the business will (or should!) consult an antitrust lawyer to check for possible antitrust problems. And every merger that combines two firms that sell competing products will be checked. Antitrust evaluation of mergers is automatic because the law requires that the merging companies file an analysis of the effects of the merger on competition along with a lot of background information so that the government can do its own analysis before the merger occurs.

> Every merger involving firms with competing products will be checked by the antitrust agencies.

What does a company have to lose if it violates antitrust law? What gives teeth to antitrust enforcement? First, in the case of price-fixing or bid-rigging, the executives involved may go to prison or the companies may pay large fines. Second, the court may break a company up (as the government proposed for Microsoft and as actually happened to Standard Oil) or limit the future business activities of the miscreant (a court order kept Kodak out of the film-processing business for many years). Third, the states and the customers or rivals suing an antitrust violator receive compensation for the harm they prove in court. A customer receives three times the actual overcharge caused by an antitrust violation. A rival losing profits from antitrust abuse receives three times the amount of the lost profit. The combination of all of these disasters that befall an antitrust violator means that most businesses are truly careful about obeying the law. Most of the cases that do make it into the courts involve either foreign companies or conduct that is a close call.

Because the cases that get into court and make the headlines are close calls, antitrust law seems confusing and difficult to many people. The Microsoft case did not dispel this confusion. The government did little to show that Microsoft actually raised the price of desktop software or impeded innovation in that market. It did show that Microsoft was out to disable its rivals. The close call in the Microsoft case is whether the harm to rivals translated into harm to consumers. After all, a company that develops a terrific product and sells it at a low price harms its rivals, if they can't match the quality and price. But the company has not remotely violated antitrust law.

Antitrust in e-Markets

Companies running e-markets need to pay close attention to all three branches of antitrust law. In case there was any doubt on the point, the Federal Trade Commission has started an investigation on the subject. And there is a large amount of informative experience in existing e-markets, where major antitrust cases have been resolved in airline reservations systems and in the Nasdaq electronic stock market.

Collusion

The biggest danger to competition in an e-market is that sellers will use the institutions of the e-market to reduce their rivalry in their customer markets or in their supplier markets. Covisint, the auto-components e-market sponsored by GM, Ford, and Daimler-Chrysler, draws the most careful scrutiny because its members compete both to sell cars to the public and to purchase components from independent suppliers. Similarly, Orbitz, the travel e-market sponsored by airlines that account for 80 percent of U.S. air travel, will need to assure the government that it will not breed collusion and raise airfares as a byproduct of its activities. Companies like eBay that have developed e-markets from scratch to serve large numbers of users are unlikely to attract attention in the same way. On the other hand, eBay is such a large player in the Internet auction market that it is likely to fall under the magnifying glass of section 2 of the Sherman Act, just as Microsoft has. And a big player like eBay will trigger a tough investigation if it tries to acquire direct competitors in the online auction business, where section 7 of the Clayton Act protects competition.

When rivals join forces to create an e-market purchasing exchange—as the automakers have in their proposed collaboration, Covisint—there will be intensive antitrust review. The government sets forth the standards applied in this review in *Antitrust Guidelines for Collaborations among Competitors,* issued jointly by the Federal Trade Commission and the Antitrust Division of the DOJ. The central question considered in the review is the effect of the collaboration on the prices and qualities of the products sold by the collaborators. Although the guidelines are written for the case where the collaborators themselves create the venue of collaboration—as the automakers did in Covisint—the same principles would apply in the case of an exchange built by an independent company where there was a danger that competitors might use the exchange to harm purchasers or suppliers.

The government's review goes beyond considering the exchange or other collaboration as a whole. If there is one feature of the collaboration—say, a reporting system where each member can find out the prices paid by other members—the review will consider that feature separately. If the feature is not needed to achieve the benefits of the collaboration, the government will challenge the feature in court as an antitrust violation, even though the rest of the collaboration is acceptable.

It is much safer for companies that have small shares of the market to work together in a purchasing or marketing exchange than for a group that collectively dominates its market. Covisint is attracting a lot of attention because its members account for more than half of the car market. If Honda and Nissan started a similar project, the review would be less stringent. The government sets the general threshold that collaborations involving less than 20 percent of the market are presumed to be okay.

> Competing companies may work together if they have small shares of the market.

A government investigation of an exchange will reckon its benefits against its dangers. The benefits are the reductions in purchasing or sales costs that the participants will enjoy and pass on to their customers. The dangers are reductions in the effectiveness of competition that will result in higher prices to customers and lower prices paid to suppliers. To survive the investigation, a proposed exchange involving rivals must show that it does more than depress suppliers' prices, even though its members generally pass the benefits of those lower prices on to customers. The source of lower customer prices must be greater efficiency—lower costs in making and executing deals with suppliers and better matching of suppliers to producers. The guidelines insist that the efficiencies show in real data, rather than be merely a suggestion of theory.

The danger to suppliers when producers purchase through an exchange like Covisint is that the producers will act together. By presenting a united front to the suppliers, they can extract a lower price than if they competed with each other. Suppliers benefit from the ability to pitch their products to a number of producers separately. If the producers purchased components jointly, the situation would be just as bad as if there were a single producer in the industry. So the first antitrust rule of an exchange is that there must not be joint purchasing by producers who together account for a significant part of the total market. The

20 percent market-share threshold might be a reasonable cutoff for joint purchasing.

Antitrust is most concerned with explicit cooperation among producers, such as joint purchasing, but it is also concerned with implicit cooperation. Tire makers might find that, although each automaker conducted its own tire-purchasing program through an exchange, all the automakers insisted on the same low price. The automakers could enforce this policy if each knew the prices paid by the others. As a result, in the case of exchanges such as Covisint that are operated by producers whose collective market share is high, antitrust considerations will force transactions to be opaque. To pass antitrust muster, these exchanges will need to demonstrate convincingly that there is no leakage of information about transactions from one producer to another. The government has strict rules already about the type of information that may be passed through an industry association. Rules equally strict will apply to exchanges.

When an exchange is owned by its major participants—the case with Covisint and Orbitz—the suspicion of illicit movement of information to the detriment of suppliers or customers will be much greater than it is for independent exchanges. Antitrust review of exchanges affiliated with producer-participants will look for stringent structural isolation of the exchange from the day-to-day businesses of the participants.

In some industries, B-to-B exchanges may create opportunities for collusion among the suppliers. Collusion will diminish competition and raise the prices paid by the purchasers. The rules of an exchange should prohibit important suppliers from bidding jointly. Secrecy regarding the prices and other terms of supply agreements is important on the supply side as well.

Antitrust enforcement is equally concerned with behavior on exchanges that might elevate prices paid by customers. The airline industry, with a long e-market track record, serves as a laboratory for studying this issue, to be examined later in this chapter. All of the dangers of collusion already discussed in connection with purchasing apply equally to selling. The most basic antitrust principle is that firms in the same market must not sell their products jointly but instead must compete for business independently. Joint selling of almost any kind will limit customers' ability to extract the best deal from sellers, and so joint selling results in higher prices than would occur under independent competition. The condemnation of joint selling by rivals is so strong in antitrust law that there is no exception for low market share. It is illegal for two competing firms to agree to set the same price, for example, even if they are tiny fish in a big pond.

Experience in the Nasdaq e-market, also discussed later in this chapter, shows how sellers try to jack up prices by using information about the prices set by their rivals. Again, on antitrust grounds, it is desirable to make an e-market completely opaque by keeping prices and other transaction terms secret.

Collusion does not always take the form of an agreement among sellers to set a common high price instead of competing with each other. Another abuse is an agreement to allocate customers to sellers.

Single-Firm Antitrust Abuses

The Microsoft antitrust case involves single-firm issues. The government accused Microsoft of trying to disable Netscape in the browser market and kill off Java. Consumers suffered, in the government's theory, because Java could have developed into a rival to Windows in the desktop operating system market. With that rivalry, the price of Windows would be lower and its quality higher. And computer users would have the choice of running their programs under Java.

Only big players like Microsoft can run afoul of this branch of antitrust law. There is effectively a blanket exemption for sellers that account for less than about 40 percent of the sales in their markets. Single-firm antitrust law focuses on preventing monopolization of markets and does not forbid acts that raise prices even though a number of sellers remain in the market. In the other two branches of antitrust law, it is illegal to make contracts or mergers that raise prices by more than an insignificant amount. But in the case of single-firm abuses causing substantial price increases, no challenge is possible unless the abuser is already a monopolist or has a good chance of becoming one. Many economists, including myself, disagree with this limitation in antitrust law.

Why are courts so cautious in condemning single-firm misconduct? Courts are worried about the use of antitrust charges as a business tool. Some people have interpreted the Microsoft case as the result of Netscape's successful lobbying effort to get the government to help protect Netscape from Microsoft's competition. There is a long history of bad antitrust cases instigated by companies that hoped to get courts to limit competition. Robert Bork has written a famous book called *The Antitrust Paradox* about the danger that antitrust law will be turned on its head to become a tool for limiting rather than promoting competition.

In one famous bad case, American color TV manufacturers accused their Japanese rivals of predatory pricing—setting prices so low that the Americans would be driven out of the market. The Supreme Court rejected this theory, observing that the Japanese had set low prices for 17 consecutive years and showed no signs of raising prices, even though most American producers had shut down. The Japanese had taken the market over by producing a better, cheaper product, not by any illegal attack on their rivals. That part of the Supreme Court's decision tracks the opinions of most economists. But the Court went on to endorse the principle that all claims of predatory pricing were suspect and that courts in general should bias their procedures against these cases. Many economists would prefer a different solution to the antitrust paradox. Investigate each claim carefully. Reject ones like that of the color TV producers where rivals are trying to hijack antitrust law. But keep markets honest by prosecuting companies that have actually attacked their rivals in ways that raise prices and harm customers. Use careful research in place of a general attitude of skepticism.

Firms dominating e-markets, such as eBay, need to be careful about their dealings with their rivals. So far, no important violations of single-firm antitrust law have surfaced. The most likely source of violations comes from patents. A patent is a powerful tool to disable rivals. A company with a patent has the legal right to shut down any rival that is using the patented technology. Suppose eBay had a patent on second-price auctions. eBay could shut down Yahoo and hundreds of other auction sites that offer second-price auctions. In the aftermath, eBay could raise its prices and enjoy the fruits of a monopoly. If eBay had a valid patent along these lines, the resulting monopoly would be the legitimate pay-off to its invention. Of course, eBay did not invent the second-price auction and has never tried to patent it.

> Dominant e-market firms such as eBay need to be careful about their dealings with rivals.

But suppose eBay had tricked the Patent Office into issuing a patent on second-price auctions even though eBay knew that the patent was invalid because the invention was actually made a century earlier. Were eBay to succeed in shutting down its auction rivals by asserting an invalid patent, it would be violating antitrust law. The law forbids a firm with a substantial position in a market to disable rivals by asserting a patent against them, when the firm knows that the patent is invalid. Given the importance of business process patents in e-markets, it is safe to predict many antitrust cases with this character in the future.

Mergers and Acquisitions

The mergers that concern antitrust enforcement most seriously are those between big rivals in the same market. The law would flatly prohibit a merger of the two big airline computer reservation systems, Sabre and Apollo, because it would create a near monopoly. Mergers that concentrate a market substantially are likely to cause prices to rise significantly. The government uses market shares to screen mergers to decide which ones do not need serious investigation, generally ones where the market shares of both merging companies are below about 15 percent. The serious investigation estimates how much a merger will change prices. If the merged company is significantly more efficient than the two separate companies, prices will fall. This type of merger gains approval. If the main effect of the merger is to reduce competition and thus raise prices, the government will oppose the merger. Notice the difference from single-firm antitrust law. Two merging firms even with modest shares have to show that their action won't raise prices, whereas a single firm can do what it wants to its rivals unless its share exceeds 40 percent of the market.

Merger antitrust procedures are different from others in another important way. All but the smallest proposed mergers must be reported to the government before they occur. The government takes a quick look at the great majority of mergers and then lets them close. A few—AT&T-MediaOne, AOL-Time-Warner, and WorldCom-Sprint are recent examples—earn full investigations. If the government decides to oppose a merger, a trial before a federal judge occurs. Only courts have final power over any antitrust issue. As a practical matter, however, the government's opposition will kill a merger, as with Microsoft's attempt to acquire Intuit and WorldCom's attempt to acquire Sprint. The last important merger trial occurred in 1997, when the government sued to block Staples' acquisition of Office Depot. The government won in court.

Mergers have become frequent already among e-market players and are sure to be an important factor in the future. Merging e-markets may be able to make a more compelling case for their merger than, say, merging office-supply stores. Fragmentation of e-markets is costly to traders in those markets. Efficiencies from mergers—both to the companies and to their customers—may be more important in e-markets than in other markets. But merging e-market players that exceed the market-share thresholds of government merger review need to be ready to prove

> Efficiencies from mergers may be more important in e-markets than in other markets.

the importance of those efficiencies and to show that they over-come the reduction in competition that results from the merger.

Regulation

Regulation provides tools for stimulating competition or for off-setting the high prices that result from limited competition or monopoly. Regulation deals with problems that are beyond the reach of antitrust action. For example, no amount of antitrust enforcement would create a market where competing firms could deliver water to houses. Because it is inefficient to have more than one set of water mains, the supply of water is a monopoly (a natural monopoly). Just about everywhere, a regulator dic-tates the price of water delivered to homes.

Though direct regulation of prices remains for local telephone ser-vice and natural gas, the fashion today is for regulators to set rules to create an environment for competition, rather than setting prices. The new approach has been a huge success in long-distance tele-phone. The Federal Communications Commission (FCC) has aggres-sively enforced rules giving all long-distance carriers equal access to telephone customers. The new approach has faltered in electricity because the new rules did not open up ways to transmit electricity from the places where deregulated producers expanded output to the places like southern California where new supplies were needed.

Although brand-new e-markets such as those created by eBay, Amazon, or MetalSite remain completely unregulated, estab-lished e-markets are heavily regulated under the new model. The Department of Transportation dictates detailed rules for the huge e-market in airline tickets. The Securities and Exchange Commission sets thousands of rules for the Nasdaq e-market.

Antitrust and Regulation in the Air Travel e-Market

Air travel has sold exclusively through an e-market since the late 1970s. Computer reservation systems (CRSs)—Sabre and Apollo/Galileo are the largest, along with Worldspan and Amadeus—manage all ticket sales, whether purchased on the web, from a travel agent, or directly from an airline. The e-market volume on these systems is second only to that of the stock market. Antitrust investigations in the early 1990s revealed how e-market tools can be used to inhibit competition. Antitrust rulings and regulations have solved some of these problems, but others remain.

Part of the e-market infrastructure of the airline business is a company called ATPCO (the Airline Tariff Publishing Company), owned by a large group of airlines, including all of the U.S. majors. ATPCO collects fares from all 550 airlines of the world and provides them to computer reservation systems, travel agents, and other customers. Through ATPCO, any airline can see current and future fares of all of its rival airlines. The existence of ATPCO is a complete anomaly from the antitrust point of view. If the companies of any other industry created their version of ATPCO to share information about prices, the FTC or the DOJ would shut it down in a second. ATPCO is a relic of the days when airlines were regulated and had to file tariffs for approval before they could go into effect.

Every day ATPCO collects new fares from airlines and passes them on to its customers. Airlines analyze the data immediately to figure out how to respond to their rivals' latest actions. The DOJ's investigation in 1994 found that ATPCO provided a way for airlines to send messages back and forth in order to avoid competing with each other. According to the DOJ, the airlines

exchanged clear and concise messages setting forth the fares each wanted the others to charge, and identifying fares each wanted the others to eliminate. Through this electronic dialogue, they conducted negotiations, offered explanations, traded concessions with one another, took actions against their independent self-interests, punished recalcitrant airlines that discounted fares, and exchanged commitments and assurances—all to the end of reaching agreements to increase fares, eliminate discounts, and set fare restrictions.

A key tool that the airlines used, the government found, was to post a fare through ATPCO that could not be ticketed until the future. Travel agents could not see the fare or sell tickets under it. Then airlines would dicker by posting other fares, also invisible except to other airlines. If one airline would not go along with higher general fares, the leaders would post low fares in markets where the dissident airline did large amounts of business and had the most to lose from lower fares. The government identified more than 50 instances where this process culminated in an agreement on higher fares. One agreement between American and Delta, according to the DOJ, resulted in an increase of up to $138 for flights from Chicago to Dallas. The negotiations through ATPCO differed from the traditional backroom operation of a cartel in one important way—all of the ATPCO daily computer files were available to the DOJ's investigators.

The government's primary cure for this misuse of the e-market infrastructure was to prohibit the posting of fares that did not go into effect immediately. If an airline wants to send a message to a rival by posting a high fare, it has to take the chance that travel agents will see the fare and steer their customers to other airlines with lower fares. And posting a low fare will attract actual passengers—maybe lots of them—to seats that could be sold for more. The government also prohibited the airlines from using any of the data sent through ATPCO to communicate with rivals—all data must refer entirely to legitimate fares for passengers. For example, an airline can't invent a fare code like SCREWDL to mean that a fare is intended to punish Delta.

> Users of e-market tools will come up with unexpected and dangerous abuses.

The experience with ATPCO drives home an important lesson of e-markets I stressed earlier: users of e-market tools will come up with unexpected and dangerous uses. Developers of e-markets have to keep a close eye on how their tools are used and to modify systems that are being abused. Some types of abuse will land an e-market in deep trouble with the DOJ for antitrust violations.

Computer Reservation Systems

In the early 1970s, the airlines received approval from the government to create a unified e-market for air travel. Even then, antitrust enforcement considered the potential dangers from an e-market operated jointly by companies that were supposed to be competing with each other. The original project failed, but American Airlines created Sabre, still the largest computer reservation system, and United replied with Apollo.

Initially, these systems were closely affiliated with their parents, a factor that contributed to some of their antitrust problems. Gradually, they have drifted away. Today, both Sabre and Apollo are quite separate from American and United. In both cases, the parent airlines spun off their shares, making the computer systems fully independent companies. Pressure from antitrust enforcers and regulators was only part of the reason for the divorces. Both systems found it desirable to distance themselves from their airline parents in order to attract other airlines as customers and to assure travel agencies that they provided unbiased access to all airlines. Future e-markets started by large existing businesses—such as carmakers—may evolve in the same way.

Each airline reservation system can make reservations on any airline. The airlines pay the reservation systems a standard amount for each seat reserved. The biggest airlines created their own systems, but smaller airlines relied on Sabre and Apollo and the other systems run by their rivals. The relationship between those airlines and the reservations systems was uneasy—the same companies were rivals in air travel but supplier and customer in the reservation business.

In the late 1980s, a number of smaller airlines started an antitrust case against Sabre and Apollo. Their theory was that American and United were using their reservations systems to hobble rival airlines. The resulting reduction in competition in air travel raised fares and harmed consumers, according to the theory. And the tactics cut the profits of the smaller airlines.

The tactics hampered airlines competing directly with American and United. They included charging competing airlines more to book a seat than the amount charged noncompeting ones—as much as ten times more. Flights of competing airlines appeared farther down the displays shown to travel agents, even if those flights were at more suitable times and had lower fares. A particularly harmful tactic was to put a competing flight on the second screen of flights, because research demonstrated that many travel agents looked only at the first screen shown by the reservation system. Sometimes Sabre would not show a particularly low fare of a competitor at all.

The case was a complete flop. Sabre and Apollo paid no compensation to the smaller airlines, and the court did not impose any restrictions on their CRS policies. The court did not even examine the evidence on the tactics that the smaller airlines challenged. Rather, the court reasoned in the following way, and was later supported by higher federal courts. First, whatever American's and United's tactics, they had not succeeded in monopolizing air travel, nor was there an attempt to monopolize the market with a dangerous probability of success. The court quoted an earlier decision of the Supreme Court: "Because the Sherman Act does not prohibit unreasonable restraints of trade as such—but only restraints effected by a contract, combination or conspiracy—it leaves untouched a single firm's anticompetitive conduct (short of threatened monopolization) that may be indistinguishable in economic effect from the conduct of two firms subject to § 1 liability." Again, the standard for what one firm—say, American or United—does by itself is vastly more lenient than the standard for what a group of firms agree to do. If the smaller airlines had evidence that American and United had agreed with each other to discriminate against competing airlines in their CRSs, the case would have had an altogether different outcome. There was no such evidence.

> The standard for what one firm does by itself is vastly more lenient than that for what a group of firms agree to do.

Second, the court considered the smaller airlines' claim that there should be an exception to the general principle that a firm can use whatever harmful tactics it wants unless it is likely to become monopolist. The exception was for a firm that owns an "essential facility." e-Markets are likely to hear a lot more about essential facilities in the future, so it is worth understanding this legal concept. For example, eBay is such an important force in Internet auctions that an opponent might brand it an essential facility. Many commentators have called Microsoft Windows an essential facility, though no court has considered the idea yet.

Examples of essential facilities include a railroad bridge in St. Louis—essential to provide rail service in that area—and wholesale electric power—essential to provide retail electric service. The Supreme Court found that these were valid instances of the concept. The denial of a rival access to an essential facility in a way that preserves a monopoly is illegal under antitrust law. Thus the owner of the railroad bridge was guilty of monopolizing rail service by refusing other railroads the use of the bridge.

The appeals court in the CRS case found that the essential-facility theory did not apply to Sabre and Apollo. Neither CRS had the power to eliminate competition in air travel and create a monopoly. It was not enough that control of a reservation system gave a big airline a tool to harm its smaller rivals and to raise fares; the legal standard is more stringent.

Third, the court considered the smaller airlines' theory of "monopoly leveraging." This theory is also likely to be important in future debates over e-markets, so it too is worth understanding.

The leading example of monopoly leveraging today is the accusation that Microsoft uses its Windows monopoly to give itself advantages in related markets. For example, Microsoft has been charged with forcing computer makers to place Internet Explorer and Microsoft Network on computers, as a condition for licensing Windows for the computers. The idea is that Microsoft can use its monopoly power in the Windows market to advance its products unfairly in other, more competitive markets, such as Internet browsers and Internet service. Another example—and the legal case where the theory was born—is Kodak's use of its strength in the film market to advance its own film-processing services against rivals that do not sell film.

In airline reservations, the theory of monopoly leveraging held that Sabre's strong position in the reservations business enabled American to harm rivals and consumers in the air travel market, and similarly for Apollo and United. The small airlines hoped to carve out an exception to the principle that the challenged tactics of a single firm had to have a dangerous likelihood of creating a monopoly to fall under the ax of antitrust. The appeals court rejected this exception on the same grounds as the first: there can be no violation of antitrust law by a single firm unless the challenged tactics (discrimination against rival airlines in the reservation system) threaten to monopolize the market where the tactics have their effect (air travel). Monopoly leveraging is not an antitrust theory at all, the appeals court held, because if there is a danger of monopolization, standard antitrust doctrine condemns the tactics, and there is no need to bring in the theory of monopoly leveraging. That theory is just an unsuccessful attempt to broaden the standard for judging the conduct of a single firm. Only Congress, by rewriting the Sherman Act, has the power to change the standard.

Monopoly leveraging perplexes economists. A firm with a strong position in one market—Sabre in reservations, Microsoft in operating systems, Kodak in film—can exploit that strength by charging a high price. No principle of antitrust law stands in the way of turning a legitimate strong position in a market into high profits. Once the firm obtains maximum profit in the original market, there is nothing more to be gained from hobbling rivals by withholding the product from them. By this argument, Sabre should charge other airlines a lot of money for reservation services, but should not diminish their quality or withhold them completely. Instead of refusing to display Continental's bargain fares, for example, Sabre should have charged Continental a high price to display them.

Economists have missed something here, because dominant firms like Sabre do indeed try to hobble their rivals by degrading services or withholding them. It seems to be hard for a big, established firm such as American to run a business, Sabre, that cooperates with its airline rivals. Rivalry in the airline business is the dominant aspect of the relationship between American and, say, Northwest, one of the airlines that sued American. The rivalry poisons the other relationship, where American sells reservation services to Northwest. Contrary to the profit motive—which would call for a cooperative reservation relationship with a high price—American degraded its services. American eventually solved this problem by spinning off Sabre completely—the airline people at American no longer have any opportunity to hobble their rivals through Sabre. The decision to spin off Sabre confirms the economists' view that hobbling rivals is never the right way to extract the highest profit from a strong position in a market, and that when it happens in the real world, it reflects a management failure.

> Hobbling rivals is never the right way to extract the highest profit from a strong market position.

Regulation of the Air Travel e-Market

Though the private antitrust case against Sabre and Apollo left their tactics untouched, regulation became aggressive at the same time. The Department of Transportation regulates airline reservation systems and maintains a set of detailed rules. These remain in effect despite the complete independence of both Sabre and Apollo from their airline founders. Neither of the two dominant systems has any incentive to tilt in favor of one airline or another.

The Transportation Department's analysis supporting the rules contains one remarkably candid statement: "We recognize that one U.S. carrier—Southwest—has prospered without participating in any CRS. Southwest's ability to succeed without CRS participation stems from the unusual nature of its operations. . . . Because Southwest's experience is unique, we will ignore Southwest in the rest of our discussion of the airline competition issues." The airlines that are being eaten alive by Southwest can hardly take the same view—Southwest's role in the market cannot be ignored.

One part of the reservation system rules bars discrimination in displays. A reservation system must follow the rules in ordering the flights on a display; it may not favor its airline parent and it may not favor an airline that wants to pay for a better position. The issue of paying for display position looms large in retailing, where grocery stores and other merchants extract large payments for a favorable shelf position. It is a growing issue on the Internet—Yahoo is gradually extending and refining its system for charging other web sites for favorable positions in its search results. eBay charges more if you want your product to be listed in bold type. Every e-market that generates displays of available products will find it profitable to sell display positions.

The second major regulation bars a system from discriminating among airlines in its booking fees. Southwest cannot negotiate a favorable deal with Sabre on the basis of its unique ability to function without using any outside reservation system.

In the days when American and United controlled Sabre and Apollo and used them to hobble rival airlines, there was a good rationale for the Transportation Department's regulations. Regulation stepped in where management failed. The rationale has disappeared with the spin-offs of the two dominant systems. There is no incentive for stand-alone reservation systems to hamper any airline customer.

The primary remaining effect of the regulation of airline reservation systems is the prohibition of display bias. If the systems were deregulated, they would immediately start selling display positions. Would that be a bad thing? Or should there be a general rule that e-markets and traditional merchants may not sell display or shelf position? Economic analysis has yet to deliver a clean answer to this question. In the meantime, the general principle that less regulation is better suggests that the time has come to deregulate the air travel e-market. By the same token, regulation of new e-markets to bar display bias is probably not a good idea.

Orbitz

Orbitz, the web travel agent under development by the major airlines, is the new focus of antitrust controversy. Orbitz will take on the two dominant Internet travel agent sites, Travelocity and Expedia. Travelocity, the larger of the two, is the child of Sabre and thus the grandchild of American, so American is competing with its own progeny.

Orbitz is the collective sales arm of competing airlines. Because any collaboration among rivals might spawn collusion, the DOJ will keep Orbitz under its antitrust microscope continuously. Initial approval will require Orbitz to demonstrate effective firewalls to prevent the abuses documented in the ATPCO case. Nobody will be allowed to work for both Orbitz and an airline, for example. Contacts between Orbitz and the airlines will be monitored carefully.

Orbitz will face the same incentive to sell display positions that the old computer reservations systems face and, for that matter, that Travelocity and Expedia face. Travelocity sells positions aggressively—it commonly displays a page for a route telling you about the airline that Travelocity features for that route. It's unlikely that Travelocity chooses its featured airlines on the quality of their peanuts.

Travelocity has complained that Orbitz will be a favored player in the Internet travel agent business, and invited antitrust review on the basis of that complaint. Already, individual airlines offer special fares on their own web sites that are not in computer reservation systems and thus not available through Travelocity. Orbitz may make these special fares available through a single search engine, giving Orbitz a big advantage over Travelocity.

In tracking this unfolding controversy, one must keep in mind that the purpose of antitrust law is to keep prices low and innovation high, not to level the playing field in each market. There is a good reason why airlines keep their special fares off the computer reservations systems—they could be found too easily by business travelers in that case. Airlines want to sell high-fare tickets to the last-minute business traveler at the same time that they sell low-fare tickets to customers who have the time and inclination to search the web for last-minute bargains. A requirement that the special fares now on airline web sites be made generally available would just kill those fares.

The Nasdaq Price-Fixing Case

The other large established e-market, Nasdaq, endured public and private antitrust scrutiny in the mid-1990s. Nasdaq's troubles began when a pair of financial economists, William Christie and Paul Schultz, circulated a paper pointing out that dealers' price quotes tended to be stated in quarters, halves, or whole dollars, rather than in eighths. Just as delicatessen customers order a pound of ham, or a half pound, or a quarter pound, but not $\frac{3}{8}$ of a pound, dealers avoided quoting prices like $8\frac{3}{8}$ or $15\frac{7}{8}$. The avoidance of odd eighths occurs in essentially all markets with quoted prices and was well known before the paper appeared. The novel suggestion of the paper was that the custom of avoiding odd eighths was part of a general conspiracy to overcharge investors.

The price a dealer charges for his services is the spread, the difference between the ask price and the bid price. If you buy a stock for the ask price and sell immediately for the bid price, you have paid an amount equal to the spread. If dealers conspired to widen the spread, they would raise their earnings at the expense of investors. The conspiracy would violate antitrust law.

Would a conspiracy to avoid prices with odd eighths tend to raise spreads and harm investors? Suppose the dealers agreed to raise an ask price that would naturally fall on an odd eighth up to the next quarter and to lower a bid price in the same way. That agreement would result in wider spreads and thus higher trading costs to investors. But an agreement to avoid odd eighths could go in the opposite direction as well—to lower the ask price in some cases and to raise the bid price. There would have to be more than just an agreement to avoid odd eighths to make the conspiracy worthwhile to the dealers and harmful to investors.

But consider stocks whose spreads are only ⅛, so the bid price might be 9¼ and the ask price 9⅜. No dealer would quote the same price, 9¼, as both bid and ask price. So the agreement would result in an ask price of 9½ and a spread of ¼, twice the spread of ⅛ that investors would have paid if the dealers had not conspired. The agreement to avoid odd eighths would definitely increase the spread. This factor means that there might be some merit in the claim that an agreement to avoid odd eighths would harm investors and raise dealer profits.

The Christie-Schultz paper launched two investigations, one by financial economists and one by the government. Economists found the Christie-Schultz approach to be roundabout. If there was an agreement to raise spreads, why not look directly at spreads? Moreover, it makes sense to look at spreads as percentages of the stock price. If the spread is 2 percent of the price, it means that an investor buying $10,000 worth of the stock will pay $200 in spread costs for the purchase and later sale. (The investor might also pay $20 or $40 in commissions, but the spread is the bulk of the trading cost.)

The Christie-Schultz conspiracy theory makes a sharp prediction: percentage spreads should be greater for stocks where the quotes are stated ¼s in comparison with those where either the bid or the ask contains an odd ⅛. What actually happened on Nasdaq during the period when the conspiracy was supposedly active? In the first group, stocks where the quotes typically included one with an odd ⅛, the average spread was $.30—some stocks at $.125(⅛), some at $.375(⅜), and a few at ⅝ and ⅞. In the second group, the average spread was $.65, a little more than twice as high.

A single key fact undermined the Christie-Schultz claim of a conspiracy to raise spreads by moving stocks into the second group. The average price of the stocks in the first group was about $9.50, while the average price in the second group was twice as high, $19. Average percentage spreads were about the same in the two groups. It's tricky to measure average percentage spreads, because the averages are sensitive to fallen angels—stocks whose prices have fallen close to zero. Their spreads are huge in percentage terms. The average spreads, including those of fallen angels, are 5.0 percent in the odd-eighths group and 4.5 percent in the second group. On the other hand, the average percentage spread measured as the average dollar spread divided by the average stock price, is 3.2 percent for the odd-eighths group and 3.4 percent for the other group. This measure is less sensitive to the fallen angels. As a general summary, I would say that the percentage spreads are close to the same in the two groups.

The key prediction of the Christie-Schultz conspiracy theory failed in the data. Few economists accepted the pair's claim to have found the footprints of a conspiracy to cheat Nasdaq investors. Instead, spreads in Nasdaq tend to be related to the level of stock prices. Higher-priced stocks have wider spreads. Percentage spreads tend to cluster around 3 percent. Stocks with prices below $10 are quoted with odd eighths, whereas those with prices of $20 or higher are quoted in quarters or halves.

The data do support one proposition—stocks with spreads of a quarter are much more frequently quoted at, say, 39¼ bid and 39½ ask, rather than at 39⅛ bid and 39⅜ ask. The market acts as if prices could be only on tick points: 39, 39¼, 39½, and so on. Prices tend to move from one tick point to another, even though there is no rule against quoting between ticks. But the tendency for prices to fall on tick points does not result in higher spreads, as the evidence shows.

Many stock markets use decimal rather than fractional prices. The United States is joining this movement. In decimal markets, such as the London Stock Exchange, the tendency for prices to fall on tick points is no less strong. In London, stock prices are quoted in pence (⅟₁₀₀ of a pound) and typical stock prices are around 300 pence. Prices cluster in multiples of 5 and 10 pence. The human tendency to seek tick points is irresistible. Even data from the census on people's ages show pronounced bunching at multiples of 5 and 10 years. It is safe to predict that every e-market will develop natural tick points where prices will bunch. No conspiracy should be read into this finding.

Though Christie and Schultz's charge that there was a conspiracy to raise spreads in Nasdaq encountered heavy sledding among economists, it received a friendly reception at the government agencies responsible for policing the stock market: the Department of Justice and the Securities and Exchange Commission. Close on their heels came the class-action lawyers, who won many millions of dollars of fees for themselves and the potential for a few dollars of rebates to millions of investors. Any e-market as large and successful as Nasdaq should be prepared for similar attacks. Poor antitrust compliance procedures cost Nasdaq huge sums of money. Nasdaq did not make adequate use of economists to defend the charges, either.

> Every e-market will develop natural tick points where prices will bunch.

The government soon forgot Christie and Schultz's indirect evidence of conspiracy when it found amazing direct evidence. Many dealers routinely taped all telephone calls to avoid later disagreements with customers. The tapes revealed a common practice of browbeating among dealers to widen spreads. In colorful language that couldn't possibly be quoted here, one dealer would call up another who had narrowed a quote and threaten retribution if the dealer didn't back down. The government's litigators couldn't believe their good fortune. The discovery of the Nasdaq tapes ranks with the Microsoft emails, the videotapes showing lysine makers conspiring to set high prices, and the ATPCO messages, as answers to the antitrust prosecutors' dreams.

Armed with this juicy evidence, the DOJ made the major market makers in Nasdaq promise to stop activities that might support an agreement to widen spreads. The agreement itself was declared illegal, and the dealers promised not to follow the agreement, without admitting that there had ever been an agreement. More significantly, the dealers set up antitrust compliance programs to prevent contact with rival dealers of the type revealed in the phone tapes. The court order formalizing the DOJ's requirements blocks many practices that appeared in the tapes, such as threats to retaliate against dealers who narrow spreads.

The DOJ's case against the dealers bought the Christie-Schultz theory about avoiding odd eighths. The DOJ ignored the lack of support for the theory found by economists (I pleaded with the DOJ legal team at the time to get in touch with the economists at the SEC who were familiar with the operation of Nasdaq, but no contact occurred through July 1995). Nonetheless, the browbeating in the tapes was not good for the investor, so eliminating it was a step forward.

The puzzle in the DOJ's case against Nasdaq occurs frequently in antitrust. On the one hand, the accused conspirators are caught red-handed soliciting each other to raise prices (spreads in the case of the dealers). On the other hand, their actions don't leave any visible mark on prices. The DOJ did not attempt to show that the dealers actually widened spreads, only that they tried. The DOJ's later case against Microsoft had the same structure—voluminous evidence that people at Microsoft were out to crush Netscape and other rivals, but little to show that Microsoft actually got higher prices or stifled innovation.

Class-action lawyers sued the dealers on behalf of investors who were the victims of the dealers' spread-raising activities. Whereas the DOJ was interested only in stopping those activities, the private lawyers were out for money. Investors were entitled to triple compensation for the higher spreads they paid, and the lawyers were entitled to fees for their legal work. Taking advantage of the explosive evidence on the tapes, the lawyers extracted remarkably large amounts of cash from the dealers. All of the dealers settled before trial. The total settlements exceeded a billion dollars. They took the form of negotiated percentages of the total volume of trades with the public. To show that antitrust lawyers have a sense of humor after all, the percentages for the first half dozen settlements were numbers that ended in fractions with odd eighths.

The dealers paid over a billion dollars in settlements despite the lack of evidence about the widening of spreads resulting from their conspiracies. The prospect of paying such large sums should deter not only Nasdaq dealers but also participants in all markets from engaging in any activities that might look like conspiracies to raise prices through contacts with rivals. From the start, e-market participants should install the kinds of antitrust compliance that the DOJ forced on the Nasdaq dealers. It's a huge mistake to wait for an investigation.

> e-Markets should pay close attention to antitrust compliance.

The SEC took a much wider approach to the abuses revealed by the investigation triggered by Christie and Schultz. Its investigation culminated in a detailed report, in extensive changes in the rules governing Nasdaq, and in about $15 million in fines on dealers.

The SEC found it suspicious that the dealers placed orders in Instinet on terms more favorable than those they offered to traders in their quotes. A dealer using Instinet to rebuild inventory might post a limit order there offering to buy at $37\frac{3}{16}$, when it was quoting to buy from traders in general at $37\frac{1}{8}$. The SEC (and the DOJ) identified this practice as a sign of collusion among dealers to keep the quotes wide. But there is another, less sinister explanation: as chapter 5 noted, dealers are careful in setting their quotes because of the possibility that an order might come from a trader with brand-new inside information. Buying from an insider at $37\frac{3}{16}$ might be a loser, because the insider is selling on the basis of new adverse information. Far fewer traders on Instinet have this kind of information, so it is safe to post a higher price. Instinet does not permit individual investors to trade on its system—traders must be institutions or dealers. The SEC did not consider research on the economics of the determination of quotes in its condemnation of the dealers. It proceeded by brute force to require that dealers' orders on Instinet and other electronic order books appear as quotes in the Nasdaq system.

A related change occurred in the way limit orders are handled in Nasdaq. Before the price-fixing investigation, dealers made instant money from customer limit orders with prices inside the quotes. For example, if a dealer was quoting 23¼ to sell a stock and 23 to buy it, and a customer placed a limit order to buy at 23⅛, the dealer could buy from another customer at 23 and sell to the limit-order customer at 23⅛ at a profit. The SEC decided this was unfair to the customer who sold at 23, given that there was another customer willing to buy at 23⅛. So it imposed a new rule—that a dealer receiving a limit order inside its quotes had to display the limit order as if it were a quote. To continue the example, the dealer, upon receiving the limit order to buy at 23⅛, would change its ask quote from 23¼ to 23⅛, and the customer who would have sold at 23 under the earlier rules now sells at a better price, 23⅛. The dealer no longer extracts a spread at all; it just matches the limit order from one customer to the buying desire of another customer.

The SEC ignored an important side effect of the rule on customer limit orders: these orders are usually for 100 shares or a few hundred at the most (limit orders for fewer than 100 shares are exempt from the rule). Before the new rules, dealers' quotes were good for several thousand shares in most cases. Customers desiring to make fairly large trades could learn the terms available by looking at the quotes. Now many quotes are hidden by customer limit orders. There is no display of available terms for larger blocks of stock.

A third change in Nasdaq's rules put into effect after the price-fixing investigation was to cut the tick, or minimum price increment, from ⅛ to 1/16 for stock prices over $10. If the earlier tick had been preventing a stock from trading with a spread smaller than ⅛, this change would result in lower spreads for that stock.

The SEC's objective in the new rules was to shrink the spreads in Nasdaq. Since the rules went into effect, spreads in high-volume stocks have fallen substantially. Many forces combined to shrink the spreads. Trading volume grew tremendously, stimulating more efficient operation. As a pure e-market, Nasdaq enjoyed huge cost reductions from cheaper computers and telecommunications and from better software. And the new trading rules probably contributed as well.

The zero-profit principle governs Nasdaq. Nasdaq has 550 registered dealers. And if being a dealer became more profitable, there would be more—there is no barrier to becoming a dealer. Once a member, a firm can start making a market in a particular stock on a day's notice. Stocks like Microsoft with large trading volumes have 50 or more active dealers, whereas small stocks may have fewer than 10 (if a company cannot attract at least 3 dealers on the average, it has to stop trading on Nasdaq). Profit is the driving force. The last dealer in to a particular stock makes just enough revenue from its spreads to cover the costs of making the market—salaries and Nasdaq quote fees.

When trading rules change to cut spreads, some dealers previously just breaking even begin to incur losses. They stop making markets where they can't make a profit. With fewer dealers and less competition, spreads widen. In the new equilibrium, the zero-profit principle holds again. Much of the effect of the SEC's attempts to shrink spreads by rule changes was probably offset in this way. The great bulk of the actual decline in spreads probably comes from other sources.

When the SEC changes the rules in a way that raises efficiency, the zero-profit principle calls for a reduction in spreads. The various changes that have moved trading to electronic order books have contributed to higher efficiency. It is less costly for some investors to find each other electronically on Instinet or another electronic order book than to trade through a dealer as an intermediary.

Lessons for e-Markets from Nasdaq

Nasdaq is the largest e-market in the world. Studying its evolution and interaction with the legal and regulatory systems of the United States is mandatory for designers of e-markets, because similar experiences will surely occur in new e-markets as they develop.

> Participants in an e-market are likely to try to conspire if they think they can get away with it.

The first lesson is that the participants in an e-market are likely to try to conspire to raise their incomes if they think they can get away with it. Conspiracy breeds most virulently when the same groups of people—airline fare setters and Nasdaq dealers—interact with each other day after day. They will use the communications infrastructure of an e-market to subvert the market. e-Market designers need to build in a high level of monitoring from the start, rather than wait for scandals to erupt. In both the airline and the Nasdaq settings, conspirators left electronic footprints but did not think that anybody would ever check the files or tapes for those footprints. They need to understand otherwise from day one.

A second lesson is that a scandal with the appearance of overcharging the public will bring heavy-handed regulation as well as antitrust trouble. Regulators often ignore careful economic analysis of the effects and side effects of their actions. They go for direct action. It's terribly important not to give them this opportunity.

e-Markets for New Cars

Regulation of established e-markets such as computer reservation systems and Nasdaq seems feather light in comparison with the regulation of potential e-markets, notably that for new cars. The promise of this e-market will remain unfulfilled unless there is a dramatic change in regulatory politics.

Every carmaker drools over the Dell model. If it weren't for regulation, you could design your own car on the Internet and have it shipped directly from the factory in a week or two. Not only could you choose from the wonderful variety of options already offered through dealers, but the system would support many new options as well. Compare the limited range of computers available at CompUSA with the incredible range at Dell's web site.

The trouble with the Dell model is that the dealer has no role in it. Unlike computer dealers, car dealers have serious political clout. Long before the Internet, dealers lobbied state governments to keep carmakers out of the retail end of the business. The dealers have pushed through protection of their retail role against the possibility of direct sales through the Internet. Although a number of web sites offer new cars, they get the cars from dealers, who absorb a considerable fraction of the benefit of the e-market.

Carmakers are working on plans for a modified Dell model, where the customer can test-drive cars at dealers and receive their cars there. These plans are likely to be diluted by the dealers, who would prefer that the Internet be nothing more than a way of developing sales leads rather than a true e-market.

> Politically powerful interests that would be displaced by an e-market can block the development of the market.

The lesson from the failed e-market for cars is that politically powerful entrenched interests that would be displaced by an e-market can block the development of the market. The car dealers have had complete success in lobbying state governments. Others may get help from the federal government. Citizens cannot always rely on the government to keep e-markets free and open— we need to keep constant pressure on our representatives to achieve this important goal.

TAKEAWAYS

- **Collusion is an ever-present danger in e-markets.** Customers or suppliers will use the communications facilities of an e-market to limit competition and harm sellers or purchasers.

- **Dominant e-market participants may face antitrust challenges even if they do not collude.** The case against Microsoft, for example, rests entirely on the company's dominant role in operating systems. eBay dominates the consumer auction market to such an extent that its business strategies might face similar scrutiny, though none has been suggested to date.

- **Mergers may inhibit competition and be challenged by antitrust agencies.** The law on mergers permits the agencies to disallow mergers on the broad grounds that they will tend to raise prices paid by customers.

- **Traditional e-markets—airline reservations and Nasdaq—have attracted heavy-handed regulation.** The Department of Transportation regulates the details of computer reservations systems. The Securities and Exchange Commission is equally involved in the operation of Nasdaq.

- **The Nasdaq price-fixing case illustrates collusion that can arise in e-markets and shows how the government is likely to respond.** Tape recordings reveal how the dealers got in touch with each other to try to raise spreads. The government extended regulation and imposed penalties, despite meager evidence that the attempted collusion actually affected prices.

- **Politically entrenched interest groups such as car dealers may use regulation to inhibit e-markets.** In almost all states, it is illegal to sell new cars on the web. Sales of other products such as wine are restricted as well.

8

Patents and Copyrights

You own what you create. An author owns the sentences in a book, a webmaster owns the appearance of a web page, a songwriter owns a song, an inventor owns a new product or process. These ownership rights provide the incentive for creative activity. Patents and copyrights formalize the rights. As the owner of a patent or copyright, you have complete control over the economic exploitation of what you have created. You can start a business based on your patent and block competitors from using your process or making your product. Or you can license your patent to any number of companies at whatever the market will bear. You can publish your own book or song, or license the copyright to a publisher or performer, again at whatever the market will bear.

These intellectual-property rights interact with e-markets in two important ways. First, methods for running e-markets can be patented. The government has issued thousands of business methods patents for e-markets and e-commerce in the past few years. Two e-market patents are famous and controversial: Amazon's patent on one-click shopping and Priceline's patent on the name-your-own-price model. Second, e-markets trade products that are protected—or should be protected—by copyrights. Music is the most prominent today, but books, videos, and software are coming.

The Value of a Patent

Patents protect inventions, not ideas. An application for a patent has to show that the invention actually works and accomplishes some useful purpose. When software running on general-purpose computers began to replace special-purpose physical equipment, the patent system resisted extending patent ownership rights to inventions embodied purely in software. The inventor of the desktop calculating machine received a patent, but software to provide the same capabilities on a computer could not. Gradually—over a great deal of resistance—patents came to cover software. A related extension included methods for running businesses. In e-markets, the two converge, because the business methods are embodied almost entirely in software.

> Patents protect inventions, not ideas.

Before issuing a patent, the U.S. Patent and Trademark Office satisfies itself on four points:

1. **Is the invention useful?** The inventor has to show that the world needs the invention. A patent application includes a section where the inventor describes an unmet need somewhere in the economy and how the invention meets the need.
2. **Is the invention new?** The inventor has to disclose what she knows about "prior art"—similar methods already in use. The inventor does not have to search to find prior art, but the Patent Office does some searching.
3. **Is it truly an invention, or is it something that anybody in the field would have**

come up with? The Patent Office will not issue a patent for a method that is obvious.

4. **Does the application teach adequately how to use the invention?** A patent is a deal between the inventor and the government—the inventor receives the patent right in exchange for disclosing the invention to the public.

The Patent Office puts a moderate amount of effort into digging out the answers to these four questions. In the process, the office relies on the truth of the inventor's application, without independent verification. But the issuance of the patent is not the last word in checking out the patent. If a patent turns out to be valuable, somebody who doubts that the patent meets the standards can start a case in federal court to put the patent to a much more rigorous test.

The court test harnesses the power of the adversarial system. The company that questions the patent—usually because it does not want to pay royalties to use the method—has the incentive to dig out information unfavorable to the patent. The owner, on the other hand, has the incentive to provide even more favorable information than was in the original application. A federal court and jury then decide whether the patent is valid. The court and jury do not have the final say, as a special appeals court for patents can overturn the decision of the trial court. The multistage system for determining the validity of patents is vastly more efficient than checking out every patent application—most patents have little value, and it would be a waste of resources to investigate them carefully.

A case called *State Street Bank v. Signature Financial* in 1998 established the legal principle that you can patent a business method embodied in software. The business method involved the operation of mutual funds in a hub-and-spoke model, so that what was really a single fund could be presented to different kinds of investors as different funds, with different charges. Since the case was decided, the Patent Office has issued almost 2,000 patents of this type, including the controversial Priceline and Amazon patents.

The owner of a patent has the right to go to court to prevent anyone else from using the method covered by the patent. Thus Amazon sued Barnes and Noble to block its one-click shopping model, and Priceline sued Expedia to block its use of the Priceline customer posted-price model. One way to obtain value from a patent is to use it to provide a unique feature for your own business. Amazon's and Priceline's cases against primary rivals are presumably motivated by the belief that one-click and name-your-own-price are features that add substantially to the values of their own businesses.

The other way to extract the value of a patent is to license it to one or several players in a business. Independent inventors without the wherewithal to create businesses around their inventions capture the value through licensing. The inventor of the variable-speed windshield wiper made a killing by licensing the invention to the auto industry rather than trying to start a new car business based on his invention. Amazon licensed its one-click patent to Apple, so Amazon is pursing a combination of both strategies for extracting value from patent rights.

The Priceline Patent

The government issued patent 5,794,207 to Walker Asset Management in August 1998. The inventor is Jay Walker, the founder of Priceline, together with two co-inventors. Priceline sued Microsoft and its now independent travel web site, Expedia, for using the patented method. Before the court could determine the validity of the patent, Expedia agreed to pay Priceline to license the method. Presumably Expedia—in the hands of top-drawer patent lawyers—made the agreement because it believed that there was a good chance that the court would find the patent valid.

A patent has two main parts. One is a manual showing how to use the method. The manual focuses on what is called an embodiment—an example of how to run a business by means of the patented method. The Priceline patent describes the Priceline business, as we know it, along with some extensions that have not yet appeared. The purpose of the manual is to disclose enough about the invention so that someone else could build a business based on it.

> The patent's claims determine the patent owner's rights.

The manual does not determine the patent owner's rights. If another business—such as Expedia—uses a method similar to Priceline's, the legal question is not whether it has copied the method described in the manual. The manual is only an illustration.

The second part of the patent—its claims—determines the owner's actual patent rights. The rights are much broader than just the right to prevent somebody from building a business following the manual.

In most patents, the first claim is the central one, which the owner hopes will survive later challenges. It stakes out the broadest definition of the method and blocks the largest set of rivals. Other claims are present in case the court later decides that the broad claim does not stand up.

Claim 1 of the Priceline patent reads as follows:

A method for using a computer to facilitate a transaction between a buyer and at least one of a plurality of sellers, comprising:

inputting into the computer a conditional purchase offer which includes an offer price;

inputting into the computer a payment identifier specifying a credit card account, the payment identifier being associated with the conditional purchase offer;

outputting the conditional purchase offer to the plurality of sellers after receiving the payment identifier;

inputting into the computer an acceptance from a seller, the acceptance being responsive to the conditional purchase offer; and

providing a payment to the seller by using the payment identifier.

Any business model that included each of these elements
would fall under the Priceline patent, no matter what other elements it also included. You can't avoid the patent by adding features to your system that Priceline does not have. On the other
hand, if you could figure out a way to run your e-market without
one of the elements in the list, you would escape from the patent.

A group of airlines, including United and American, have
launched a Priceline competitor called Hotwire. In the Hotwire
model, the customer describes a round-trip, including the days of
travel but not the times. The customer can limit the number of
stops on each leg and can opt against overnight flight. Immediately after receiving this information, Hotwire responds with a
price. The customer has 30 minutes to accept the price.

The Hotwire model has some of the advantages of Priceline
that are discussed in chapter 6. Because the customer does not
know what airline is offering the price, one airline can use
Hotwire to make a sneak attack on a rival, without the rivals
finding out the low fare by routinely checking Hotwire. And
Hotwire excludes business travelers in much the same way as
Priceline does—by requiring the passenger to accept stopovers
and departure times dictated by the system and not necessarily
convenient for the traveler.

Comparing the Hotwire procedure to claim 1 of the Priceline
patent suggests that Hotwire is safely outside that claim. The
customer does not make a conditional offer, but just a nonbinding inquiry. The customer does not provide credit card information as part of the inquiry, but only when she has accepted an
offer made by an airline. Hotwire does not send the conditional
offer to airlines, but queries the airlines about the fares they
want to offer for a particular trip. Airlines do not accept offers
from customers; they make offers themselves.

On the other hand, Expedia's model has several of the elements of claim 1. In Expedia, you specify the price you are will-

ing to pay as a binding offer—the conditional purchase offer in the first element. You provide credit card information as part of the conditional offer, as in the second element. It is possible that Expedia then transmits your offer to airlines, as in the third element. I say "possible" because Expedia might decide itself what offers to accept, in which case the transmission to airlines required in the third element might not occur. Similarly, the last two elements may not be present in the Expedia model. Priceline has another patent, 6,134,534, where the conditional offer is compared to rules stored in a database rather than transmitted to the seller for evaluation.

In any case, Priceline is convinced that Expedia falls under the Priceline patent. On October 13, 1999, Priceline sued Expedia and its former parent, Microsoft, for infringing the Priceline patent and for a variety of other misdeeds. According to Priceline's complaint, Microsoft had lengthy negotiations about a partnership using Priceline's technology—the patent and trade secrets relating to patents not yet issued. Instead of following through on the partnership, according to the complaint, Microsoft started a similar business in Expedia. Microsoft tells the story a rather different way, of course. But Microsoft and Expedia's willingness to pay for a license suggests that they saw the possibility that the court would rule in Priceline's favor.

A company called Marketel has sued Priceline on the grounds that its employees actually invented the Priceline model and should own the patent. Priceline even faces a dispute about its ownership of the slogan "Name Your Price!" Another company has sued Priceline, claiming ownership of the slogan.

The Amazon Patent

Amazon owns a patent, 5,960,411, covering its one-click ordering model. The first claim of the patent reads as follows:

A method of placing an order for an item comprising:

under control of a client system,

displaying information identifying the item; and

in response to only a single action being performed, sending a request to order the item along with an identifier of a purchaser of the item to a server system;

under control of a single-action ordering component of the server system,

receiving the request;

retrieving additional information previously stored for the purchaser identified by the identifier in the received request; and

generating an order to purchase the requested item for the purchaser identified by the identifier in the received request using the retrieved additional information; and

fulfilling the generated order to complete purchase of the item

whereby the item is ordered without using a shopping cart ordering model.

Before Amazon received the patent, Barnes and Noble's online bookstore had a feature called Express Lane, permitting orders with a single click. Amazon got the patent in September 1999, sued Barnes and Noble in October, and persuaded a federal court to prohibit the single-click model from the Barnes and Noble web site in December 1999. So much for the idea that the wheels of justice grind slowly.

It is hard to see how a web seller could offer anything like single-click ordering without falling under the Amazon patent. Barnes and Noble complied immediately with the court's order by adding another step to Express Lane, requiring that the customer confirm the order. In this way, it avoided the central element claimed in the patent, a single action by the customer.

The court has not yet determined the validity of Amazon's patent. The challenge will probably focus on the third item in the patent checklist—whether one-click shopping rises above an idea that would occur to almost any web store designer. If Amazon passes the second checklist item, that no web seller offered one-click service at the time Amazon filed for its patent, then Amazon's case on the nonobviousness of the one-click model will be reasonably strong. Barnes and Noble's best shot is to show a good example of one-click shopping prior to Amazon's patent application.

The Value of a Copyright

A copyright gives the owner control over writings, music, photographs, movies, videos, or art. Control is limited to the prevention of copying. A copyright protects the creator's expression rather than the substance. A copyright on a cookbook means that another cookbook can't copy the recipes, but it does not stop a restaurant from using a recipe for free. A copyright is easy to obtain—just write the word copyright, the date, and your name on your work and you have one. It isn't even necessary to put in the © symbol. You do not need to apply to the government to enjoy a copyright.

Copyrights are distinctly secondary to patents in protecting the creators of e-markets. An e-market web site has copyright protection for the appearance of its web pages and for all written material about the site. The information that customers contribute to an e-market web site is not protected by copyright. eBay tried to prevent BiddersEdge from copying auction results on the grounds that eBay owned a copyright on the results, but the court rejected the theory. Generally, courts have determined that compilations of data from customers do not enjoy copyright protection. I'll return to this dispute shortly.

> Copyrights are distinctly secondary to patents in protecting the creators of e-markets.

Copyrights are hugely important in e-markets in a different way, because digital products—MP3s, e-books, videos, and software—can be protected by copyright. A new law passed by Congress in 1998 spelled out procedures for copyrights for digital products.

The Digital Millennium Copyright Act

The copyright law always prohibited the copying of works without the permission of the owner of the copyright. It is flatly illegal to sell copies of a CD, for example. Although pirate CDs are a problem in countries such as China, they are not a big drain on the U.S. music industry. It is fairly easy to root out illegal CD factories in the United States. Pirating of digital copies, on the other hand, is hard to control without some new tools. Any modern personal computer can rip digital music off a CD and make copies of the resulting MP3 computer file. Music joined computer software as a digital product vulnerable to widespread copying and distribution without the permission of owners. e-Books and videos will join them in the near future.

The old copyright law left uncertain whether it is legal to provide technology that helps other people copy protected works. Owners have challenged new technologies throughout history. Sellers of sheet music wanted to banish scrolls for player pianos, the earliest digital product. The movie industry wanted to ban the VCR. The music industry imposed limitations on the digital audio tape recorder and now wants to hobble Internet-based technologies that assist the exchange of digital music, most of which is copied from CDs whose copyrights are held by the industry.

The new copyright law, the Digital Millennium Copyright Act, or DMCA, resolved doubts about copying protected digital works in an ingenious and constructive way. On the one hand, it excuses a broad class of players from any general responsibility for copying done by their customers using their facilities. An Internet service provider is not to blame for pirated digital music that moves through its system. On the other hand, the DMCA places a high level of responsibility on all companies whose products may be involved in handling digital works.

The key provision of the DMCA in the second respect is this: *No person shall circumvent a technological measure that effectively controls access to a work protected under this title.* Once the owner has used a technology that could be effective, everyone involved in handling digital works has to let the technology do its job.

Two types of technology control access to digital works: watermarking and encryption. A digital watermark is the electronic equivalent of a paper watermark. Subtle alterations in the patterns of bits, way below the threshold of hearing or vision, show who owns the music, picture, book, or video. The watermark is everywhere in the digital file—you can't remove it by taking out a piece of the file. Software easily detects and reads a watermark even though humans aren't aware of them.

The DMCA would require Napster to check MP3 files exchanged through the Napster system for copyright notices embedded as digital watermarks. Unless the user copying a file could show permission from the owner, Napster would block the exchange. The same obligation to check for watermarks would fall on hardware and software for managing MP3 files and playing them, either on computers or on pocket MP3 players.

Digital watermarks would solve the problem of music piracy in the same way that the illicit copying of books at Kinko's and other copy shops came to an end. It is illegal for a shop to help copy a book bearing a copyright notice unless the copyright owner consents. The key to the marking approach to protection is the use of an easily detectible notice of a copyright. Kinko's does not have an obligation to research the copyright status of every document customers bring for copying. But it does have an obligation to honor a copyright notice. Similarly, if digital music had copyright notices as digital watermarks, Napster would have the obligation to check for these notices and to bar unauthorized copying of marked MP3 files.

The DMCA commands three general types of businesses to block users from circumventing copyright protection: (1) sellers of user hardware, (2) sellers of user software, and (3) web sites that facilitate the exchanging of files. Of the three, hardware provides the most traction. Almost all hardware comes from big legitimate companies that follow the law scrupulously. Their disk drives, audio boards, and portable players will check for copyright watermarks as soon as the music sellers activate the DMCA's anticircumvention provision by watermarking their music. It's not practical for an underground business to gain much volume in these lines. It takes manufacturing facilities, distributors, and retailers to sell hardware profitably. Once a business has this high a profile, it has no choice but to obey U.S. law.

User software is a distinctly secondary line of defense for copyrights. Computer makers would be sure that the software shipped on new machines would comply with the law, and so would legitimate above-ground software vendors. Playback software from Microsoft, Apple, or RealNetworks would check for copyright watermarks. But, if there were an opportunity to help people pirate copyrighted music because hardware detection was not in place, underground software for that purpose would spring up right away. Because software is a purely digital product easily distributed over the Internet by small organizations, enforcement of the anticircumvention law is much tougher for software than for hardware. And the same holds for Internet web sites. More than 100,000 sites offer illegal copies of music already, despite the constant efforts of music owners to shut them down.

Enforcement of anticircumvention law is much tougher for software than for hardware.

CDs are the primary source for MP3 files of digital music. To gain the protection of the DMCA, the music industry needs to put watermarks in CDs. Then all music ripped from CDs would contain the watermark, which is almost impossible to remove without seriously degrading the music. The industry has adopted a standard for digital watermarks, but seems to be years away from putting it to use. On the other hand, watermarks are widely used in digital images. Software like Adobe Photoshop looks for watermarks when loading a new file.

Almost nobody understands the DMCA's framework for establishing effective ownership rights through copyright marking. Everybody jumps to the conclusion that protection means encryption. CDs are not encrypted, but DVDs are. You cannot rip the digital content from a DVD and make copies, because the content is scrambled and requires a secret password to unscramble it. Most people assume that music CDs need encryption to make copyrights effective.

The entire existing stock of CD players and CD drives on computers would become obsolete if music CDs began to be encrypted. Sales of new music would suffer during the many years before the stock of CD players turned over and most people had new equipment capable of playing encrypted CDs. Because the CD is technologically obsolete already, it is safe to predict that we will not see an encrypted CD. Encryption will wait until music distribution moves to a new technology, most likely the digital download over the Internet.

Encryption enjoys the same status as watermarking under the DMCA—it is illegal to sell hardware or software that circumvents copyright protection by decoding encryption. The problem with the encryption approach to controlling illicit copying is that decryption is purely a software function. Experience with DVDs demonstrates how hard it is to make encryption work. The movie industry won a court case against a web site, 2600.com, that distributed software called DeCSS for cracking and ripping DVDs. Outside the courtroom, hawkers offered T-shirts bearing the nucleus of the computer code for cracking DVDs. The code circulates widely on the Internet, and there is no way to suppress it.

Music and other digital works will achieve the highest level of protection through a combination of watermarking and encryption. Record companies should start watermarking CDs immediately. Watermarking and encryption should be used for music sold as downloads.

The music industry's approach to copyright effectiveness has ignored the framework of the DMCA. Instead of taking the steps to trigger the protection of the DMCA—watermarking or encryption—the industry wages war on new technologies. This reaction from an established industry is nothing new. The movie industry came within one vote on the Supreme Court of banning the video cassette recorder. And the music industry's attack on the digital tape recorder did not get what it sought—its outright elimination from the market—but did win limitations on the new technology.

Napster and other pioneers of distributing digital works on the Internet became the target of the music industry in 2000. The case against Napster was the same as earlier cases against new technologies—Napster's users were copying music without the permission of copyright owners. Napster sought the shelter of the DMCA, which clarifies the role of service providers by shielding them from prosecution as long as they comply with the anticircumvention law. Because the music industry did not watermark digital music, Napster did not help its users circumvent an effective protection technology. Hence the DMCA permits the operation of a web site like Napster. There was no more justice in shutting down Napster than in blocking the sales of the hardware that people use to copy and play MP3 files. If Napster is illegal, then so is the sale of disk drives and audio boards, technologies also widely used in copying and playing music ripped from copyrighted CDs.

Media coverage of the Napster controversy never touched on the central issue: the music industry could have started watermarking CDs many years ago, in which case Napster would have both a legal duty and a practical method for controlling the use of its technology for copying protected music. Instead, Napster came across as a hero in counteracting the high prices of CDs and distributing free music widely, to some people, and as a villain disregarding the property rights of music owners, to others. Those who believe firmly in enforcing property rights, but defended Napster as the wrong victim, did not get their message across. The beautiful logic of the DMCA and the music industry's stubborn refusal to make use of it remain a secret.

Ownership of Web Data

e-Markets generate lots of data. In the Nasdaq stock market, you can see the order book at Island or Instinet containing hundreds or thousands of orders at any moment for each of thousands of stocks. Hundreds of Nasdaq dealers post quotes that change every few minutes or seconds on thousands of stocks. Amazon displays data collected from its customers on sales rank and also publishes reviews contributed by customers. eBay displays about 5 million auctions at any one time. The data are either the centerpiece of the business model (Instinet or eBay) or an important adjunct (Amazon).

Who owns data collected from customers? Regulators and courts are in the process of resolving this tricky question. For Nasdaq, the Securities and Exchange Commission makes rules about access to the order books. For eBay, a federal judge made a preliminary ruling about the rights of other web sites to copy data from eBay.

eBay's Auction Data

BiddersEdge is a web site that aggregates auction data from other auction sites. It does not run auctions itself. You can ask BiddersEdge to show you all the auctions for 1889 silver dollars. But the results will be mostly from Yahoo, with a few from lesser auction sites. Mighty eBay is not included. You have to press a button labeled "Check this category at eBay," which transports you to eBay. A court found—in a preliminary manner—that eBay has property rights in its customer data. eBay has refused to license BiddersEdge to copy the auctions, though Yahoo and others are happy to see BiddersEdge promoting their auctions.

> A business cannot copyright data compiled from customers.

A well-established principle holds that a business cannot copyright data it compiles from customers. Instead, the legal principle behind the BiddersEdge decision was that a property owner has the right to keep trespassers out of its property. eBay has the right to block BiddersEdge from copying 5,000,000 auctions by visiting eBay 100,000 times a day because it costs eBay significant resources to transmit so much data to BiddersEdge. With BiddersEdge at work, eBay has to enlarge its server capacity or accept degradation of its service. The court saw BiddersEdge as stealing computer services from eBay, in effect.

eBay is struggling with BiddersEdge over network effects. Internet auctions create strong network advantages. Sellers want to list their auctions in a way that is visible to the maximum number of potential bidders. Buyers want to search in the place with the maximum number of auctions. eBay, the first and always the largest consumer auction site, has captured the network advantage. eBay's model for the auction business calls for all customers to use eBay, meaning that eBay would capture all the profit available in the business.

BiddersEdge hoped for a different model for the auction business. Numerous auction sites would compete to list auctions. Users would see all sites as roughly equal, because all would be aggregated in BiddersEdge. All purchasers would go first to BiddersEdge to find the most promising auctions to bid in. BiddersEdge would capture the profit available from the entire auction business by charging auction sites referral fees.

eBay had no interest in helping BiddersEdge capture profits as an aggregator of eBay's and other auctions. Without an aggregator playing the role BiddersEdge aspired to, eBay would continue to aggregate the auction business itself. The two companies have negotiated extensively to see if BiddersEdge could pay enough to offset eBay's losses from dilution of its aggregation role. No deal has worked—eBay needs more compensation than BiddersEdge could realistically pay.

BiddersEdge collects auction data the same way that web search engines do, through software called a spider that visits auctions sequentially and copies data about them. Spiders or robots have been part of the web since its inception. The Internet has a Robot Exclusion Standard that permits web authors to mark pages as off-limits to robots. Major search engines such as Google respect these markings, contained in robots.txt files. BiddersEdge ignored them prior to the court order. Notice that the effect of the court's action is effectively to require that robots follow the Robot Exclusion Standard. There is a nice parallel with the DMCA, which requires web sites and other players to respect electronic copyright notices.

There is nothing new or surprising about the principle that a web site can control who is allowed to see a web page. The Internet is not a library open to all visitors. Many commercial sites restrict entry to parts of their content to those with accounts and passwords. It would be a violation of securities law, for example, if OffRoad Capital let all visitors see information about pending deals—by law, this information can go to only a limited group of existing customers, who have been properly screened.

The court's determination that eBay had the right to exclude BiddersEdge provoked an outcry from experts on Internet law. A group of 28 specialists, including Lawrence Lessig, famous from the Microsoft case, filed a friend-of-the-court brief opposing the theory that the operator of a web site had the power to control who visits the site. The brief does not consider whether it should be permissible for a site to limit visitors to those with passwords, but seems to uphold the idea that a web page accessible to individuals must also be open to robots. Oddly, the brief does not even mention the Robot Exclusion Standard. Its logic suggests, in effect, that the standard should be dropped in favor of an Internet-wide policy that all sites must welcome robots.

The friends' brief argues that the Internet fosters competition by helping customers compare prices. Aggregators and shop bots serve this interest. The new legal principle from the eBay-BiddersEdge case would permit sites to defeat shop bots and thus prevent price comparisons. eBay and other sites have an incentive to defeat these activities. To keep markets as competitive as possible, web sites should let robots copy any page they offer to the public.

The brief takes a short-term view. Basically, it argues that the auction user benefits from BiddersEdge's aggregation of auctions from the existing set of auction sites. It does not consider market equilibrium under different rules about access to auction data. In this and earlier chapters, I have noted that the personal auction business has powerful network effects. As a result, a single organization—eBay, BiddersEdge, or another—will become the focal point of the auction business. Either most auction business will occur on eBay—the current situation—or most auction purchasers will find auctions through an aggregator—BiddersEdge's hope. The court's endorsement of eBay's right to exclude Bidders-Edge makes the eBay-centric model more likely. The brief's proposed rule forbidding discrimination against robots opens the door for the model focusing on an aggregator such as Bidders-Edge. It's a question of one monopolist against another, not a question of monopoly against competition. The brief fails to make a strong economic case that the antidiscrimination rule would deliver permanent benefits to the consumer.

The brief's assumption that spiders searching for good prices all over the Internet make markets significantly more efficient and competitive seems naïve. After all, the first principle of e-markets is to conceal your best price from humans. Nobody would show a best price to a spider! Even in the limited markets, such as books and CDs, where prices are posted to the public, customers flock to Amazon rather than using mySimon to track down the significantly better prices that are available at BooksAMillion or AlphaCraze. And BooksAMillion does not post its best prices by any means; it operates a membership club that gives individuals lower prices based on their cumulative purchases.

Piggyback Web Sites

BiddersEdge uses a robot to aggregate data from multiple sites. Because aggregation is useful to users, BiddersEdge provides a service. The court's decision to bar BiddersEdge from intruding on sites such as eBay's that do not welcome the intrusion involved a balancing of the value of the aggregation service against the cost imposed on eBay.

The issue of robot intrusion also arises when the intruder does no more than duplicate the function of the host. In that case, one site repackages the services of another. A piggyback site adds nothing new to consumer choices; it merely exploits services actually provided by others. Among shop bots, the leader, mySimon, has sued Priceman.com to prevent it from copying mySimon's price search results and presenting the results as a Priceman product.

The strongest case in favor of the right to block robot intruders from a web site is in the piggyback situation. No added service is lost when piggybacking is outlawed. Incentives to create useful services such as mySimon are improved if these services have the right to defend themselves against piggybackers if they are successful.

TAKEAWAYS

- **Patents must satisfy four criteria: usefulness, novelty, nonobviousness, and full disclosure.** The Patent Office makes a preliminary determination whether a patent meets the criteria, but the ultimate determination occurs in federal courts if a patent turns out to be valuable and is challenged.

- **If a business model uses all of the elements of a patent claim, it is covered by the patent.** Even if the model includes other features not considered in the patent, the new model cannot be used commercially without licensing the patent.

- **Copyrights protect expression, not ideas or function.** Copyrights provide important protection for music, videos, and books traded in e-markets. They do little to protect business models themselves.

- **The Digital Millennium Copyright Act created a practical system for protecting music and other download products.** If the music industry included digital watermarks in CDs, then the provisions of the act would prevent other businesses such as Napster from helping people exchange copyrighted music.

- **Operators of e-markets have the right to exclude others from copying their data.** The Internet's Robot Exclusion Standard allows a web site such as eBay's to determine who can visit the site. A recent case has given the standard the force of law.

9

The Future of
e-Markets

e-Markets will grow in coming years and will spread to many new applications. Some established independent e-markets will flourish, including eBay, Nasdaq, and computer reservations systems. In almost every industry, established players will buy inputs and sell products online through their own captive e-markets or through those of their suppliers or customers.

e-Markets will bring dramatic improvements to economic efficiency. Many of the benefits will flow to the users of e-markets. Consumers benefit from access to greater varieties of collectibles at eBay and from the ease of selling unwanted items, both without paying high margins to stores or dealers. Consumers benefit from the convenience of online purchasing of the growing variety of retail products sold on the web. Businesses operate at higher efficiency by routing purchases and sales through e-markets as well. New procurement models permit a wider variety of suppliers to bid to become suppliers. Online sales cut the costs of managing sales. Most of these efficiency benefits at the B-to-B level will result in lower prices to the consumer, because competition among sellers translates cost reductions into price reductions. e-Markets will contribute to the growth of the standard of living in coming decades.

In the past, consumers captured most of the benefits of innovations, not the businesses inventing them or putting them to first use. Innovation brought steady rises in the public's standard of living, not ever-growing fortunes for the innovators. When everybody can copy new ideas without having to pay for them, they spread widely, and the public, not inventors, benefits from them. Without an incentive to invent and develop, though, the supply of new inventions may be small. Patents and other forms of intellectual property enable inventors to capture parts of the values of their inventions. Patents strike a compromise between the goal of rewarding inventors and the goal of widespread adoption of new technologies to raise the general standard of living. They give inventors the power to charge for the use of their inventions for a period of about 18 years. Inventors also derive some protection through copyrights and trademarks, by keeping their ideas secret, and from the advantage of being first to market. All forms of protection are temporary—after a few decades, every new technology becomes essentially free.

> The stock market values new technology when it has patent or other protection.

The stock market values new technology to the extent that a corporation owns patents or has some other form of protection. Ideas themselves do not generate value in the stock market; value comes from the stream of income that the ideas will generate in the future. The stock market shows the value of what a corporation *owns*. When a patent protects an innovation, corporate value in the stock market reflects the profits that the company will earn from its monopoly in the patented technology, together with the income that it will earn from licensing the patent. Similarly, the stock market values the advantage of being first to a market to the extent that the advantage translates into profit stretching into the future. Looking at the stock market is helpful in understanding the future of e-markets because investors commit their wealth on the basis of their projections of future profit.

Stock Market Valuation of e-Market Companies

The stock market reveals the *present discounted value* of the earnings of a company. The market reveals the consensus about the value today of the future profit, with discounting to take into account the lower value of future dollars. Four factors determine the present discounted value of the stream of profit that a corporation earns from its technology, first-to-market advantage, and other unique features:

- the level of profit currently earned,
- the growth rate of profit in the near term,
- the number of years before growth finally ends and the company has a stable share of a stable market, and
- the discount rate the stock market applies to future profit.

Current profit. Measurement of current profit is a challenge for e-market firms. Reported profit understates true profit because accountants deduct many development costs along with current expenses in reckoning profit. Amortization of these development costs over future years would give a better picture of actual profit. On the other hand, these firms pay many workers and suppliers with their own stock, and a proper accounting would count these expenditures against profit—an accounting procedure that high-tech firms have resisted mightily. A reasonable principle is that profit is a fraction of revenue, in the range of 5 to 30 percent. The profit percentage varies across business models. In pure retail, where the e-market player buys finished goods and sells them without altering them, the percentage is low. In a pure software business, where the cost of making another copy is tiny, the profit percentage will be at the upper end of the range.

Near-term profit growth. To project profit growth into the near future, analysts look to recent actual revenue growth, based on the above assumption that profit is a roughly constant fraction of revenue. Successful e-market players enjoy stunning revenue growth. Figure 9-1 shows eBay's revenue growth per quarter for 1999 and 2000. The average rate is about 15 percent per quarter, or 75 percent per year after compounding.

Years until growth ends. Growth rates of 75 percent per year cannot last forever. Although Figure 9-1 does not show any strong indication that eBay's growth slowed over the two-year period, a company growing at eBay's rate would swallow the entire economy after a couple of decades. In 18 years, eBay's revenue would rise from its 2000 level of about $400 million to the value of the goods and services produced by the entire U.S. economy—about $10 trillion. The company's growth has to slow down. The most convenient way to express the slowdown is in terms of the number of years until growth stops. I assume that

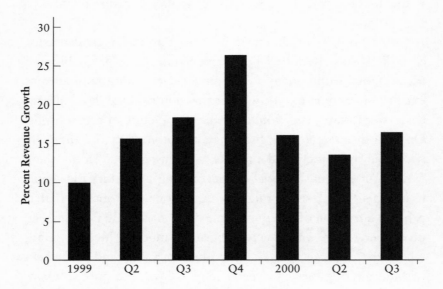

Figure 9-1. eBay's Revenue Growth, Percentage per Quarter

growth each year will fall by the same number of percentage points. For example, if eBay's growth will end in 15 years, it will be 75 percent initially, then 70 percent a year later, then 65, and so on down to zero.

The discount rate. Financial economics is reasonably confident that the discount rate for risky e-market companies is about 18 percent per year (a conclusion of the Capital Asset Pricing Model widely used for business decisions). A dollar of profit to be earned next year is worth $1/(1+0.18) = \$.85$ this year, a dollar of profit to be earned in two years is worth $1/(1+0.18)^2 = \$.72$, and so on.

Analysts often combine the last three factors into a *capitalization factor* expressing the ratio of market value to current profit. If profit does not grow, the capitalization factor is just the reciprocal of the discount rate, or about 6 for the discount rate of 18 percent. The market places a value of $6 million on a constant stream of profit of $1 million per year stretching into the indefinite future.

If profit will grow forever at the same rate, the capitalization factor is the reciprocal of the discount rate minus the growth rate. For example, if the growth rate is 17 percent, so the difference is $18 - 17 = 1$ percent, the capitalization factor is $1/.01 = 100$ and the market value of the stream starting today at $1 million is $100 million. Growth matters a lot. Notice that the formula breaks down if the growth rate equals or exceeds the discount rate. We can't contemplate the possibility of indefinite profit growth higher than the discount rate—it is the financial equivalent of traveling faster than the speed of light.

Now bring in the length of time before growth falls to zero. As long as growth does eventually fall to zero, we can calculate the capitalization factor. The calculation requires some advanced mathematics or a spreadsheet, so I will give the result as a graph. Figure 9-2 shows the capitalization factor with the 18 percent discount rate and 75 percent per year near-term growth rate of profit, for different numbers of years until growth ceases. The capitalization factor reaches 50 if growth lasts 11 years, 100 at 14 years, and 500 at 23 years of growth.

eBay's annual profit was about $60 million. eBay's market capitalization at the end of November 2000 was $10 billion, so the capitalization factor was 10/0.060 = 167. From figure 9-2, the corresponding time until growth ends is about 17 years. Earlier in 2000, at the time of maximum enthusiasm in the stock market about e-commerce, eBay's market capitalization was $24 billion, implying a capitalization factor of 400. The corresponding time until growth ends is 26 years. So the drop in eBay's value by $10 billion would follow from a rethinking about eBay's longer-run prospects, shortening the time to zero profit by 9 years.

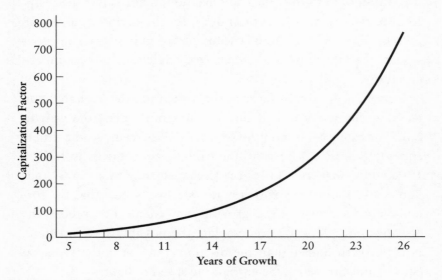

Figure 9-2. How the Stock Market Capitalizes Future Profits

Suppose a company has current profit growth of 75 percent per year. Growth will slow down over time, reaching zero in a specified number of years. Future profit is discounted at an 18 percent annual rate. The curve shows the capitalization factor—the ratio of stock market value to current profit—for different numbers of years of growth. If growth will continue for more than 20 years, even though at a diminishing rate, the capitalization factor is astronomical.

These calculations have two important implications. First, astronomical capitalization factors of 200 or 400 times current profit do not contradict the economic principles of the stock market. Instead, they require a prospect for continuation of rapid growth of profit, at gradually declining rates, for around two decades. The capitalization factors do not prove that the stock market has gone crazy, as some commentators have suggested. Second, big changes in market values of e-companies will accompany changes in beliefs about future growth that seem completely realistic given the uncertainties about the distant future. Swings in market value do not prove that the stock market responds irrationally to fads.

> Swings in market value do not prove that the stock market responds irrationally to fads.

Values of Major e-Market Companies

Many e-market hopefuls—including OffRoad Capital—are private companies whose stocks do not trade. Placing a value on these companies is largely guesswork. But a number of larger and earlier e-market players are traded on Nasdaq, including several discussed earlier in this book: FreeMarkets, eBay, Amazon, and Priceline. Two other Nasdaq companies whose values depend largely on e-market activities are the following:

- *Ariba,* which provides e-commerce software and applications services to large organizations.
- *Ventro,* which operates e-commerce sites selling specialty chemicals, instruments, and equipment to pharmaceuticals and biotechnology customers.

Figure 9-3 shows the market capitalizations of the six companies on two dates—the end of March 2000 (shown by the length of the bar) and the end of November 2000 (shown by the length of the dark part of the bar). All of the companies lost value during the period. But note the continuing high value of the larger and better-established companies at the top of the figure—Ariba, Amazon, and eBay.

Ariba

The first lesson from figure 9-3 is that well-established e-market companies with substantial current revenue and the promise of future profit command high values in the stock market. The most valuable e-market player, Ariba, achieved $279 million in revenue in 2000. Sales grew by almost 600 percent from the fourth quarter of 1999 to the same quarter in 2000. Reported

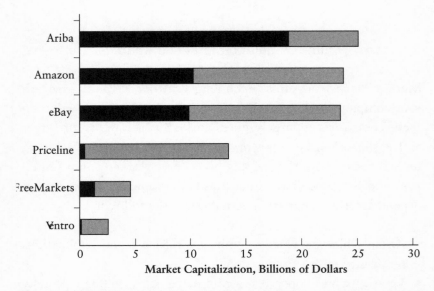

Figure 9-3. Market Capitalizations of e-Market Players, March 31 and November 24, 2000
The length of the bar shows the market capitalization at the height of enthusiasm for e-commerce, at the end of March 2000. The length of the darker part of the bar shows the market capitalization seven months later. The three leading players, at the top, retained substantial fractions of their market values.

accounting net profit, which treats all marketing expense as a deduction from profit, was negative. Because a good part of the marketing expense is investment in brand building, the company was profitable by economic standards in 2000. Analysts foresee substantial continuing growth in future years. A major high-tech investment bank predicts $3 billion or $4 billion in annual revenue by 2004 with an accounting profit rate net of sales cost of 25 or 30 percent. A reasonable figure for Ariba's economic profit is 30 percent of sales.

The stock market valued Ariba at about $19 billion at the end of November 2000. Economic profit was 30 percent of $279 million, or $84 million. The capitalization factor was 19,000/84 = 225. Growth of revenue and profit projected at the end of 2000 was about 25 percent per quarter. From the analysis underlying figure 9-2, I calculate that the stock market expects that Ariba's growth will continue for another ten years.

Earlier chapters show why Ariba is such a success. The company helps its customers run e-markets suited to their circumstances. One core market is procurement by large corporations (chapter 4). Ariba equips its customers to run their own auctions or less formal procurement operations. It competes with other software sellers, such as CommerceOne and Moai, and also with the consulting/ASP model of FreeMarkets. The other core market is sales at posted prices (with blanket discounts) from catalogs (chapter 6). Here Ariba provides software enabling its customers to sell the huge volumes of products where the benefit from dickering over individual purchases is too small to pay off.

Few recent neutral e-market startups have generated adequate volume to survive.

Ariba's efforts focus on existing businesses that are building e-market infrastructure, not on startups that hope to have a neutral role in an independent e-market. Though neutral exchanges can be successful and valuable—think of Sabre and Nasdaq—few recent neutral startups have generated adequate volume to survive.

Notice that Ariba's capitalization factor of 225 is well below eBay's of 400, even though Ariba grew much faster in 2000 than eBay did. The stock market appears to believe that rivals will overtake Ariba more quickly than rivals will overtake eBay. Ariba lacks the powerful network effects that protect eBay's dominance of the independent auction business.

Amazon

Amazon is the pioneer of the simplest e-market model, where customers buy at posted prices. The company sold about $2.2 billion in books, music, and videos in 2000. A reasonable guess about its economic profit in 2000 is 5 percent of total revenue, or $139 million. Its market capitalization near the end of the year was about $10 billion, a capitalization factor of 72. Amazon's sales grew a little less than 50 percent from late 1999 to late 2000. The analysis reflected in figure 9-2, when applied to the somewhat lower current growth rate of Amazon's profit in comparison with eBay's, shows that Amazon's capitalization factor makes sense if the growth of profit will continue, at ever diminishing rates, for about 24 years.

Amazon competes in markets where the zero-profit principle applies without question. Although there is a reasonable prospect that Amazon can earn five cents of profit per dollar of sales, its rivals will earn less. The prospective entrant to the online book, music, and video market will foresee no more than a normal return to the investment needed to launch the business. Amazon will earn its extra profit from a combination of superiorities. First, the company has a respected brand name associated with the reputation for trouble-free customer experiences. Second, Amazon built a huge base of customers in the early days when it was the only significant online retailer. Many of these customers remain loyal despite the growth of rivals offering lower prices and comparable service. Amazon is still the leader in developing features that increase loyalty, including wish lists and sophisticated recommendation software. Third, Amazon's scale conveys efficiencies in logistics in comparison with smaller operations. Online selling bears the burden of high costs of fulfilling customer orders—about 15 percent of revenue for Amazon—that hold back online business relative to big retail chains. Amazon's scale also feeds back into its first two advantages: the company achieves a higher benefit to technical improvements in its operations and so will remain the leader in web site usability and reliable performance.

Priceline

Chapter 6 found that Priceline uses an e-market model well suited to the particular needs of the airline and hotel markets. The essence of the model—the binding offer from the traveler to the airline or hotel—avoids the disadvantages to the seller of posting low prices. Priceline helps airlines and hotels fill up space that would otherwise stay empty, without compromising high prices charged to business travelers. Chapter 8 discussed the Priceline patent, which will generate revenue from rivals such as Expedia that have adopted similar e-market models. Priceline could even consider a business model based entirely on licensing its e-market technology to other travel suppliers and not operate its own travel web site at all.

Priceline's market cap collapsed despite its valuable e-market business model.

If Priceline is such a great idea, why did its market cap collapse to a paltry $400 million in late 2000? Certainly it was not lack of revenue. Priceline sold about $1.3 billion worth of air travel, hotel, and other products in 2000. If it enjoyed the same relation between revenue and market capitalization as Amazon, Priceline would be worth about $5 billion, not $400 million. Moreover, Priceline's growth of sales in 2000 was a couple of percentage points higher than Amazon's. The story of Priceline's fallen star is not a shortfall of sales.

Instead, Priceline made the mistake of pushing its e-market model into areas where it did not belong. These included long-distance phone service, groceries, and gasoline. In the case of phone service, the Priceline model adds little to what was already available—customers looking for bargains can visit many web sites and even dicker with carriers. Grocery stores already have fine-tuned price discrimination tools based on coupons and affinity cards. For groceries and gasoline, the extension into products without an existing ticketing or reservation infrastructure involved horrendous logistical problems. Although gas stations generally don't discriminate among their customers, the logistics of giving a Priceline customer a special low price proved overwhelming. Apparently Priceline wound up selling groceries and gas to its customers at prices well below those paid to the stores and gas stations.

Two big questions hang over Priceline, once it straightens out the mess caused by the unwise extension of its e-market model. One is the validity of its key patent. Its dispute with Expedia ended without legal resolution of this issue. The second question is the success of competition from Hotwire, whose e-market model—sufficiently different from Priceline's to avoid the patent—competes with Priceline. Hotwire offers another way to strengthen profitable price discrimination in the travel business. Competition is also growing from airlines' and hotels' own web sites pushing Internet specials, crafted to avoid appeal to business travelers, and from Orbitz, the travel web site sponsored by a number of major airlines.

FreeMarkets

FreeMarkets' business model received a cautious endorsement in chapter 4. The company recognizes that its customers—large businesses such as H. J. Heinz and Celanese—want to operate and control their own procurement e-markets, rather than use independent e-markets. FreeMarkets continued to grow rapidly during 2000, signing up one big company after another. Revenue grew 320 percent in 2000 over 1999, though its growth had fallen to about 17 percent per quarter by the end of the year, and analysts projected growth in 2001 somewhat below that level.

A reasonable approximation for FreeMarkets' economic profit is 20 percent of revenue, or $18 million in 2000. The company's market capitalization at year-end was about $1.3 billion, for a capitalization ratio of about 74. Figure 9-2 applies to FreeMarkets because its growth rate of 17 percent per quarter is only slightly above the rate for eBay that lies behind the figure. Consequently, the stock market values FreeMarkets on the basis of growth ending only about 11 years in the future, as against figures in the 20s for eBay and Amazon.

Chapter 4 may explain the quicker loss of advantage for FreeMarkets in comparison with the other successful companies considered here. FreeMarkets relies on expensive human beings to assist customers in setting up procurement auctions, where rivals like Perfect.com just entering the market perform the same functions with software. The Internet has shown over and over that software scales much more successfully than human effort. In addition, FreeMarkets may lose business rapidly to procurement departments, once they learn how to run their own auctions.

Ventro

Ventro's 90 percent loss of market capitalization during 2000 provides a perfect example of how perceptions about B-to-B e-markets shifted during the year. Ventro operates an ambitious neutral exchange called Chemdex. The business model calls for numerous suppliers of chemicals, supplies, and equipment to list their offerings on the exchange to pharmaceuticals makers and other customers in the life sciences business. Ventro grew rapidly in 1999, reaching about $80 million in revenue at annual rates by the end of the year. But growth stalled in 2000, as Chemdex's suppliers developed their own captive online sales operations and the customers shifted toward the captives or set up their own online procurement facilities. Ventro's gross profit—the difference between revenue and payments to suppliers—was only barely positive. Given selling and fulfillment costs, Ventro's economic profit margin was almost certainly negative.

At this writing, Ventro is seeking a buyer for Chemdex. The company hopes to join the many other suppliers of B-to-B infrastructure, such as Ariba, whose customers are established businesses. The stock market is deeply skeptical of its outlook. Ventro's market capitalization of around $100 million is way below the immediate liquidation value of the company, which is about $400 million. Stock market analysts, normally a group relentlessly optimistic about companies whose values have crashed, give little support as well.

Changes during 2000

For many e-market players, 2000 was a perplexing year. They grew rapidly, achieving or exceeding goals set at the beginning of the year. Established consumer-oriented businesses such as eBay and Amazon and B-to-B infrastructure providers such as Ariba and FreeMarkets proved and extended their business models. Yet the market caps of all of these conspicuously successful companies fell dramatically. And utter collapse befell e-market businesses with weaker or inappropriately applied business models, such as Ventro and Priceline.

In 2000, the market caps of many successful e-market players fell dramatically.

Figure 9-4 applies the declining-growth valuation model of figure 9-2 to all of these companies except Ventro (a company that does not appear to have any prospect for making profit from its sales). The length of the entire bar shows the results of the analysis for the stock market value at the end of March and the length of the dark part of the bar for the value at the end of November. All of these companies except Priceline achieved sales projections during the year, so I have used the same level of year-2000 profit and profit growth for the March and November calculations. For Priceline, I used a much lower rate of growth in November than in March because of the dramatic shortfall relative to projections that became apparent later in the year.

Figure 9-4 tells the following story: for all five companies (and for many others as well), prospects for continuing growth far into the future declined during the year. Investors became aware of the challenge to an e-market player of holding off rivals. eBay—given 26 years of profit growth by the more optimistic view in March—had retreated to 17 years by November. Notice that the writing down of distant growth prospects was least severe for Ariba and Priceline. For Ariba, the decline in market capitalization, as shown in figure 9-1, was smaller than for the others. In addition, the market already saw a relatively speedy decline in growth for Ariba. For Priceline, the collapse of growth during the year accounts for most of the large decline in market

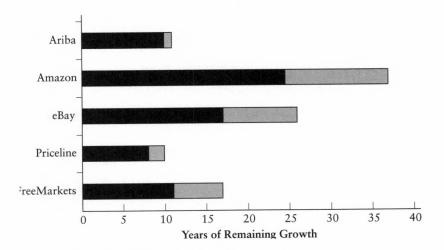

Figure 9-4. Market Perceptions about Future Growth
The entire bar shows the number of years of future growth indicated by each company's market capitalization at the end of March 2000. The darker part of the bar shows the number of years of future growth indicated.

capitalization, leaving only a relatively small reduction in the length of the period of continuing growth.

The distant future holds a great deal of leverage over the stock market. The shift to a more pessimistic 17 years of growth from 26 years cost eBay's shareholders 58 percent of the value of their holdings in just a few months. The opposite happened during 1999 and the first three months of 2000, when a shift toward optimism gave the shareholders huge capital gains. As new information about the distant prospects of e-market companies hits the market in the future, equally large fluctuations in market value will occur.

The Future

The stock market is the most reliable guide to the future of e-markets. Investors vote with their money every day about the prospects of the more mature players who trade on the stock market. Moreover, the market reveals projections of future profit that are consistent with analysis of trends in e-markets. These are the projections:

> The stock market is the most reliable guide to the future of e-markets.

The Internet auction for individual items will deliver huge and growing value to consumers and businesses. eBay owns this sector. It will continue to capture the benefits of network effects in auctions. Specialty auction sites for business equipment or surplus inventories will make few inroads into eBay's dominance of auctions. eBay will join Microsoft as the object of antitrust scrutiny.

Internet auctions for securities will continue to develop. The U.S. Treasury used electronic auctions for government securities long before the Internet. MuniAuction does huge volumes of bond auction business on the Internet, primarily as an ASP. Hambrecht, AZX, and OffRoad will expand as Internet auctioneers of equity.

Procurement e-markets will pass the trillion-dollar-per-year mark soon. The reverse English auction is the workhorse of procurement auctions, implemented by FreeMarkets as a consultant and ASP, by Ariba, CommerceOne, Moai, and many others as software providers, and by large companies with their own infrastructure. Independent exchanges will account for little of this business.

Nasdaq will continue to flourish as a neutral real-time exchange, but few other applications of this e-market model will develop. The Nasdaq model suits the fast-moving stock market, where buyers and sellers don't want to wait for periodic auctions. But there are relatively few other products where a neutral exchange is likely to predominate.

e-Markets with posted prices will continue to expand rapidly, especially for B-to-B transactions. The Amazon model is fully established for sales to consumers. There will be few opportunities to build valuable businesses on the posted-price e-market model, because of the zero-profit principle. Most of the expansion in the consumer area and virtually all in posted-price B-to-B commerce will come from established traditional companies replacing traditional sales models with more efficient Internet versions. In B-to-B, customer-specific pricing such as blanket discounts will be the rule. In consumer posted-price e-markets, price discrimination tools such as Priceline will continue to expand.

TAKEAWAYS

- **The stock market shows the value of what a corporation owns.** Unless a corporation can establish a patent or other right to its e-market model, others can copy it and the value will go to consumers, not to the corporation.

- **Market values depend on the current profit level, the near-term growth rate, the length of time when growth will continue, and the**

discount rate. A company with a good prospect for profit, a high near-term growth rate, and the likelihood for sustaining growth for five years or more will enjoy an extraordinary value in the stock market.

- **High market values for e-market players such as eBay and Ariba make sense, because their current growth rates are so high.** eBay's earnings grew at an annual rate of 75 percent in 2000 and were expected to continue to grow rapidly in future years, supporting its valuation of $8 billion at the end of 2000.

- **Declines in market value in 2000 resulted from a combination of reduced future profit levels for some players and a general change in expectations about longer-term growth for all players.** Those companies whose profit prospects faded during the year suffered the loss of almost all their value.

- **Market values and capitalization factors remain high for a number of e-market players, reflecting the value they have created.** Ariba and eBay retained around half of their high market values. Both companies had convincing prospects of positive and growing profits.

- **e-Market business models are proven in a number of areas and will continue to enjoy rapid growth.** e-Market business volume has continued to grow at rapid rates, despite lower values of e-market companies. Prospective growth remains high.

Index

Page numbers in *italics* refer to figures.

DATE DUE

Demco, Inc. 38-293